A MARRIAGE SERVICE FOR YOU

A Manual to Help the Bride and Groom Prepare A Christian Marriage Service

Robert J. Peterson

A MARRIAGE SERVICE FOR YOU

PRINTED IN U.S.A.

TABLE OF CONTENTS

Foreword 5

The Purpose of This Book 6

Preparing for Marriage 7

What Makes a Marriage Christian 9

A Marriage Between People of Different Churches 12

What Happens at a Marriage Service 14

Marriage and the Worship of God 15

The Outline of the Marriage Service 16

How to Arrange and Prepare
    Your Marriage Service 24

Some Examples of Complete Marriage Services
    The Traditional Episcopal Service 26
    A Contemporary Episcopal Service 30
    The United Methodist Service 35
    The Traditional Presbyterian Service 38
    A Contemporary Presbyterian Service 41
    The Traditional Lutheran Service 44
    A Contemporary Service
        Based on the Lutheran Tradition 49
    A Contemporary Service
        Based on the Presbyterian Tradition ... 53
    A Contemporary Non-Denominational Service .. 56
    A Roman Catholic Service 62

Marriage Service Materials Arranged for Comparison
    Calls to Worship 79
    Invocations 79

Prayers of Confession 82
Declarations of Pardon 84
Scripture Readings 84
Introductory Statements 85
Declarations of Intent 90
Vows 93
Exchange of Rings 96
Declarations of Marriage.................... 98
Prayers for the Marriage
    Prayers Asking God's Blessing
        Upon the Marriage 100
    Prayers for the Heritage of Children
        and the Well-Being of Families 107
    Prayers for Spiritual Graces.............. 108
    Prayers by the Bride and Groom 109
Beneditions................................ 110

Music for Worship and Weddings 113

Acknowledgements............................. 116

FOREWORD

This workbook has grown out of many requests by young couples for materials they could use for marriage services. I have always felt a bit uneasy reading words over the heads of young people when, even after a study of these words together, I knew they were foreign at best. This workbook is offered as a means to help couples and pastors develop services which are both Christian and personal.

I want to thank the many couples who used this workbook in partial form and who made so many helpful suggestions. I also want to thank Mrs. Hattie Sweet Bowser for the preparation of the section on music.

THE PURPOSE OF THIS BOOK

A wedding day is a great day. It is one of the highlights of a person's life, and, hopefully, remains one of the treasures we have with us all our lives. The purpose of this workbook is to help you find a deeper and more lasting joy at this special time. Marriage is a personal thing. Two people are committing their lives to each other in love, in fidelity, and in hope. The marriage service itself should reflect this personal aspect of marriage. However, marriage is also something for the families involved, and for society; therefore, the marriage service needs to reflect the understanding that life and love bear social responsibility. Marriage in our Christian faith is also part of our relationship to God. The marriage service, to be Christian, must also reflect God's will for us and for our life together.

This workbook will guide you in writing and selecting materials which will let you build a marriage service that is personal, that reflects social responsibilities, and that exhibits the marks of God's pattern for Christian marriage.

PREPARING FOR MARRIAGE

In some ways you have been preparing for marriage all your life. However, marriage itself is not the main object of life, and you should not view your wedding itself as the sole object of your future. In our religion we are taught that our main purpose in life is to give glory to God and enjoy him forever. Yet it cannot be stressed too much that who you marry is one of the two or three most important decisions you will ever make.

This is not a workbook on preparation for marriage, but it would be wrong to talk about marriage services without mentioning the importance of marriage preparation. Above all, remember that Christian marriage is a serious matter. You are making a permanent decision. Your future, its happiness, its stability, and its fulfillment, depends to a large degree upon whom you marry. There is **no** good reason to have a hasty courtship and marriage. There is no such thing as love at first sight. It is sad but true that some people spend more time preparing to buy a new car than they do in preparing for marriage.

The following is a list of the **minimum** number of things you should consider before you marry.

1. You should spend a great deal of time talking and thinking about your basic goals and expectations in life. These conversations should touch such vital areas as what is happiness, where do we want to live, how often are we willing to move, what are our financial goals, what view of religion and God do we share, what standards of right and wrong do we share. You should tell each other what you see for your life together in five, ten, and twenty-five years ahead.

2. You should meet each other's families and speak with them and discuss your relationship to the families — their expectations, and your expectations. Both families are always part of a marriage and this cannot be overlooked.

3. You should make an appointment with your family doctor and discuss with him the various methods of birth control. You should have a physical examination, and make sure that each partner knows the true physical condition of the other. You should discuss your feelings about children, and when they should become a part of your marriage. If you do not plan in this area, the chances are very good that you will become parents sooner than expected.

4. You should make a budget for your first year of married life, and you should discuss the handling of finances. This is an area of married life which causes problems unless you make sound plans.

5. You should meet with the minister who is going to perform the marriage service about three months before the marriage and counsel with him about marriage preparation.

WHAT MAKES A MARRIAGE CHRISTIAN

Having a wedding in a church no more makes a marriage Christian than appearing in a courtroom makes one a lawyer. To have a Christian marriage, the bride and the groom must bring a prior Christian commitment to the marriage.

The first thing that makes a marriage Christian is for two Christians to marry. In our present day society, religion is often considered a side issue, and many people feel that it should not play a role in true love and marriage. However, any responsible marriage counselor knows how intimately religion affects marriage, both positively and negatively. Saint Paul teaches us in 2 Corinthians 6:14-16 that we are not to suppose that we can have a Christian marriage when one of the partners is not a Christian.

The second factor in a Christian marriage is that of obedience. Obedience is owed to God, for the key to Christian marriage is building that marriage upon God's pattern. Another way to say this is to say, "God's way is the best way," because that is how we were made to live.

There are certain characteristics, certain life patterns which come out of the obedience we owe to God. The following are the basic characteristics of Christian marriage.

1. A Christian marriage is to be **holy**. Holiness means that God is interested in your marriage and that he wants to bless your life together. A holy marriage is a marriage which looks to God for strength and guidance, through both the good times and the bad.

2. A Christian marriage is to be **permanent**. There are many arguments for the permanence of marriage, the first of which is that children need the stability of a loving, permanent home for their own development. God wants the stability of a Christian home so that, through it, he may raise up Christian children. However, the Christian emphasis upon permanence also rests upon our

respect for people and human life. A wife is a person for whom Christ died. She is not a plaything to be abandoned when she no longer is of interest. A husband is also a person for whom Christ died, and he is not to be traded for a wealthier or more handsome model. Christians believe that marriage is for life, because it is only through this kind of commitment that two people can face the joys and sorrows of life, and share in bringing another human life into the world.

3. A Christian marriage is to be built upon **faithfulness**. Faithfulness certainly means sexual faithfulness. Christians believe in the joys and pleasures of sexuality, but we believe that sexuality is far more than some kind of game. Sexual relations between husband and wife produce the children, and bind the parents together in a loving and deeply personal way. Because sexuality is important, God expects us to treat it with importance and respect. Faithfulness is the cement which binds a marriage together. Christians also believe that faithfulness to our husband or wife is a discipline which delivers us from the level of the animal kingdom. Because we can know God and do his holy will, we can be more than an animal who must satisfy his desires. In Christian marriage, God makes a place for our animal desires, but they are satisfied in a way which can elevate us above mere instinct. Faithfulness means to respect each other as persons who have feelings, needs, instincts, and a great capacity for love.

4. A Christian marriage must have a place for **forgiveness**. Three of the most difficult words in any language are, "Please forgive me." To ask forgiveness and to grant forgiveness are two things which seem to strain humans more than anything else. In a marriage we have to learn to forgive one another if we are going to remain married. The saddest comment a person can make is for a wife or husband to say, "I just have to live with it, because Jim is so proud he can never say I'm sorry." We must learn forgiveness, for God in Christ has

forgiven us.

5. A Christian marriage must be based upon **love**. It is rather easy to say, especially today, that love is enough. Love is important. It is vital and two people should not attempt to build a life and home together if they do not love each other. Love is the foundation of marriage, but love is more than physical attraction. Love, to be real, must also contain the other building blocks of marriage: holiness, permanence, faithfulness, and forgiveness.

A Christian marriage is a marriage between two people who have given their lives to Jesus Christ, and who seek to obey God and his pattern of life for them.

A MARRIAGE BETWEEN PEOPLE
OF DIFFERENT CHURCHES

Normally, when two Christians are married, they are married in the bride's church by the bride's minister. However, some people would like to have another minister participate in the service, especially if that minister has a personal relationship with the couple or the family. The proper way to handle this is to ask the bride's minister to invite the other minister to participate in the service with him.

It is a sad fact that the Christian Church is not united in Christ, and so, sometimes, when Christians fall in love and seek Christian marriage there are barriers between churches. In most cases, permission may be obtained for a joint marriage service, where the ministers of both churches participate. If such an arrangement is contemplated, it is proper to arrange permission so that both ministers share in the service. Normally the minister in whose church the marriage will take place arranges for the kind of service to be used.

If there is to be a marriage between one partner who is a Christian, and one who is not, then there are several alternatives the couple should consider. They may be married by an official of the state. They may be married in a Christian service if the non-Christian partner can conscientiously take those vows. The couple can be married in a non-Christian service, if the Christian partner can conscientiously take those vows. There is also the possibility of having a blessing of the marriage after a secular or non-Christian marriage.

A marriage between a Christian and a non-Christian should not be entered into lightly. Not only because of the biblical passages such as 1 Corinthians 7:12-24, and 2 Corthians 6:14-7:1, but because of the difficulties encountered when two people holding different values and goals in life are married. It is important to share the same religious faith in a marriage, because our religious faith shapes our values, our self-understanding, and our outlook on marriage itself.

WHAT HAPPENS AT A MARRIAGE SERVICE

On the surface it seems rather silly to ask what happens at a marriage service. It is rather plain to see. Two people are married and the minister signs the license. This is true, at least as far as the state views things. The marriage service is a legal ceremony in that it confers legal rights and a certain legal status upon people. However, this is not the point we are concerned with here.

In terms of our Christian faith, the basis of a marriage service is a covenant. Two people make a covenant between themselves and God. The covenant is an agreement based upon promises. The heart of a Christian marriage service is the exchange of vows in the presence of God. The Church, normally represented by the minister, symbolizes the presence of God. The vows or promises of Christian marriage are normally set within the context of worship. Marriage is a personal event for the people involved, but it is also a public event, an important public event, for the community and for the church. Since marriage is so important the marriage service should be dignified and formal enough to express, in a meaningful way, the seriousness of the occasion.

MARRIAGE AND THE WORSHIP OF GOD

The exchange of vows in a marriage is set within the worship of God. Since marriage is not a private affair, it is set within the context of public worship. This is often underlined when, during the regular Lord's Day service, a bride and groom will exchange vows. This same understanding carries over to the marriage service held at some other time.

Since Christian marriage is set within the context of worship, there are certain understandings which must be observed.

1. A marriage is not a show and must never be treated as such.

2. The same attitude toward music, appointments, and behavior appropriate to the worship of God on Sunday applies to a marriage service.

3. The appropriate place for a marriage is the house of worship, and, under normal circumstances, a Christian marriage should be held there.

4. The materials, readings, outline, and vows must be in line with Christian beliefs and the normal standards for worship in the congregation.

THE OUTLINE OF THE MARRIAGE SERVICE

Just as there is no one God-given order of worship, so there is no one set order or outline for a marriage service. One of the ways in which you can make your marriage service meaningful and personal is to select those elements of Christian worship which will best express your commitment and joy. However, there are certain basic elements which must be present to have worship be Christian, and also have marriage be Christian.

The basic elements which ought to be in every marriage service are these:

1. A statement or reading by the minister of the meaning of marriage, and the meaning of this service. This may be portions of Scripture, an introductory statement, or a short homily.

2. A prayer asking God to be present and to look with favor upon this service.

3. The exchange of vows. These vows must be said aloud by the persons being married, or said aloud by the minister and assented to by the bride and groom, publicly and verbally. These vows must include the understanding that this marriage is to be built upon holiness, permanence, faithfulness, forgiveness, and love.

4. A prayer and blessing asking God to help you fulfill your vows and build your home within the covenant in Christ.

In many Protestant churches, these basic elements of the marriage service are set within the framework of a worship service. This service is called a prayer service or the service of the Word, and it includes prayers, Scripture readings, a sermon or homily, and a public affirmation of faith. Many Protestant churches, and all Catholic churches add to this service of the Word, the service of the Sacrament or Communion. If Communion is served, it ought to be a public Communion. Communion ought to be open to all those who would normally take

Communion, not just the bride and the groom. In some Protestant and in all Catholic churches, marriage is considered a sacrament along with the other sacraments of the church. In most Protestant churches, marriage is considered a holy institution, but it is not considered a sacrament along with the sacraments of Baptism and the Holy Communion. Because of this, some Protestant churches will not serve communion at the time of a marriage.

The following are typical outlines for marriage services. The first is a short outline and it would be appropriate for a private wedding involving only a few people.

I

Introductory Statement
Declaration of Intent
Invocation
Vows
Exchange of Rings
Prayers
Benediction

The second outline is a simple service which could be used for any type or size of wedding. Normally a service like this will last ten or fifteen minutes. The outline includes more worship elements, but the participation of the congregation would be limited.

II

Prelude
Processional or Processional Hymn
Call to Worship
Invocation
Scripture Reading
Homily or Introductory Statement
Declaration of Intent
Vows
Exchange of Rings
Declaration of Marriage
Prayers

The Lord's Prayer
Benediction
Recessional or Recessional Hymn
Postlude

The third outline is that of a marriage service set within the service of the Word in Christian worship. This service will last anywhere from twenty to forty minutes, depending upon the length of the sermon, and the types of responses chosen. This outline will allow the congregation to take part, but under normal circumstances it will also require that a wedding bulletin be prepared so that the congregation can follow and participate in the service. The participation of the congregation in the marriage service is most desirable, for it delivers the service out of the category of show and underlines the family and communal aspects of marriage.

III
Prelude
Call to Worship
Processional Hymn
Prayer of Confession
Declaration of Pardon
Response or Psalm
Old Testament Lesson
Response
New Testament Lesson
Homily
Affirmation of Faith
Declaration of Intent
Vows
Exchange of Rings
Declaration of Marriage
Prayers
The Lord's Prayer
Hymn
Benediction
Recessional

The fourth outline shows how a Communion service

should be included in a marriage service, if it is desired and permissible. A Communion service must always be seen as a service of and for the whole congregation and not as a private affair. In line with this, it would be imperative to make the service the worship of the whole congregation and include the things necessary for worship and Communion in your church.

IV

Prelude and Processional

The Service of the Word

(This would include the lessons, sermon, creed, etc., required in your church.)

Introductory Statement

Declaration of Intent

Vows

Exchange of Rings

Declaration of Marriage

Prayers or Pastoral Prayer

The Service of the Sacrament

(This would be conducted according to the rite of your church. The Lord's Prayer would normally come after the prayer of consecration. The final prayer of thanksgiving should include a thanksgiving for the wedding and a blessing upon it.)

Hymn

Benediction

Recessional and Postlude

The following is a list of worship items and notes which will help you understand the various parts of the marriage service. While these items appear in the order in which they are normally used, they may be used in varied ways. However, any worship service should proceed in a logical manner. You would not begin with a benediction and end with an invocation.

Prelude — This is usually musical. It may be instrumental or vocal. The prelude is presented to help members of the congregation turn their thoughts to God and to this particular service of worship.

Processional — This may be a hymn sung by the congregation or a piece of instrumental music. During the processional, the wedding party enters the sanctuary.

Call To Worship — Normally this is a verse or two from Scripture which sets the mood or context for the worship service.

Invocation — This is a prayer in which we ask God to be present and to look with favor upon this service.

Prayer of Confession and Assurance of Pardon — In Christian worship, it is always proper and highly desirable to begin worship with a prayer of confession. This prayer is an acknowledgment that without God's help and forgiveness, we cannot live as his people. The assurance or declaration of pardon is normally drawn from Scripture and it is the assurance that God will forgive us and receive us when we turn to him.

Psalms and Responses — One of the traditional and beautiful ways to praise God and show our response to his majesty is to respond with a Psalm. It could be read by the minister, or in unison by the congregation. Often Psalms are read responsively by the minister and the congregation. If there is a musical setting, the Psalm could be sung. Psalms can be used as a response to the declaration of pardon. They can be used as a response between Scripture lessons. A Psalm is traditionally followed by the **Gloria Patri**. There are many ways to use Psalms and other responses in a worship service, but in general they serve to beautify the service, and they give the congregation a way to express its response to a part of worship. The **Gloria Patri, the Gloria in Excelsis**, a Psalm, a verse from a hymn, a solo, even an appropriate piece of instrumental music can serve as a response. The use of various types of responses can allow you to express many of your feelings and thoughts for the marriage service.

Scripture Readings — It is always appropriate and

normally desirable to have the minister or a member of the wedding party read one or more selections of Scripture which tell about the Christian understanding of marriage. These lessons could be an Old Testament reading, a New Testament reading, a reading from a Gospel, or a reading from an Epistle. Any music which is used as a response to a Scripture lesson ought to be appropriate to the meaning of the lesson.

Homily — A homily is a short sermon. It is to be based upon the Scripture lessons read, and it often takes the place of the introductory statement.

Affirmation of Faith — It is proper that, when Christians gather for worship, they confess their faith together by using a creed or an affirmation of faith. The Apostles' and the Nicene Creeds are the ancient creeds and are used most often. The Nicene Creed is the creed most often connected with the Communion service. The creed should be recited or sung in unison by all the congregation.

Introductory Statement — The introductory statement is a short, formal statement about the meaning of marriage and the service about to take place. In the past it has contained a public announcement asking if there are any reasons why the marriage may not take place. This part, as well as the publishing of the banns is now often omitted, for the Church is no longer the custodian of public records it once was. If you desire an informal introductory statement, you should ask your minister to use a short homily and then discuss with him the various things you would like to have mentioned in the homily.

Declaration of Intent — In marriage services it is traditional and desirable to ask for a formal declaration of intent. This is a question to the bride and the groom asking if they are willing to be married, and if they come to be married of their own free will. The declaration in intent often includes the giving of the bride in marriage by the father. This giving of the bride should be seen as the formal consent and acknowledgement of the marriage by the families involved. This of course could take other forms. In a Christian marriage, the giving of the bride does not imply that a bride is the property of either the father or the groom. In some modern marriage services the entire declaration of intent is omitted, because it is presumed that the minister has determined this intent beforehand.

Vows — The vows are the heart of the marriage service. These form the solemn covenant between the bride, the groom, and God himself. As was said above, these vows must include the understanding that this marriage is to be built upon holiness, permanence, faithfulness, forgiveness, and love. In the Catholic Church, the word consent is used to signify the vows of marriage.

Exchange of Rings — The ring is our cultural symbol of marriage, and it is normally given as a sign of the vow or promise. Logically the giving of the ring must follow the marriage vows. Often the minister offers a prayer or blessing for the intention symbolized in the ring. Today you should, under normal circumstances, have a ring for both the bride and the groom, or have no rings at all. A man ought to be as willing to wear a wedding ring as the woman.

Prayers for the Marriage — One of the privileges we have as Christians is that we can ask God's divine blessing upon our lives and our union in marriage. Prayers after a marriage need to reflect our joy, our concern that we will fulfill the vows made, and our petitions that God will help us and guide us. One meaningful and beautiful way to handle these prayers is for the groom and the bride to offer a short prayer themselves followed by a prayer by the minister. Normally these prayers are concluded with the Lord's Prayer.

Declaration of Marriage — This is a formal statement that the two individuals are now husband and wife. This declaration is often concluded with a phrase or verse of scripture concerning the permanence and holiness of marriage.

Benediction — The benediction is a blessing given by the minister which concludes the marriage service.

Recessional — When the wedding party leaves the sanctuary, you may have a hymn sung by the congregation, a recessional march played on the organ, or any material which will allow the participants to leave the sanctuary in an orderly and dignified manner.

Postlude — The postlude is music which is presented to let the congregation leave the sanctuary in a mood of worship and reverence.

HOW TO ARRANGE AND PREPARE
YOUR MARRIAGE SERVICE

1. Read through pages 26-78 in this workbook. Here are several complete marriage services. Observe how the various worship elements are combined. Observe the outline.

2. Read through pages 79-112 where you will find materials arranged for easy comparison.

3. Make up an outline of the various items you would like to have in your service. Arrange them so that they follow a logical order.

4. You will notice numbers in the outer margins of the pages in these sections. The numbers are for your use. They can be used to identify parts of the service you may want to insert into your outline.

5. If you want to write parts of your service instead of selecting items from this book, then write them in full into your outline.

6. After you have your outline finished and your material selected or written read pp. 113-115, the section on music. You may want to confer with your organist, soloist, or other musicians on the music listed there or other music. Write into your outline the music to be used.

7. After you have your service arranged, make an appointment with your minister. He will go over the material and help you with further arrangements. Your minister will help you plan the physical arrangments in the church: where people walk, stand, kneel, sit, and the like. You may have to modify your outline a bit to conform to the physical arrangements of the church.

8. Remember that your minister wants to help you, so if he has suggestions about the service you have arranged, listen to him and take his advice to heart. If he must say no to something you truly want, please honor his judgment. Ministers are normally reasonable people.

9. You may, if you choose, select one of the complete

services, pp. 26-78 in this workbook. If you so, you will still have to adapt it to the physical requirements of your church.

10. If you want the congregation to participate in the service, it is best to have wedding bulletins prepared, and then have the ushers distribute them. Usually the church office can take care of this and arrange for a mimeographed or printed bulletin. A wedding bulletin can be a very good way to underscore the worship aspect of a marriage service. It is also a great help to those of your guests who would not normally know the worship procedures of your church.

11. Blank pages for notes and your outline are included in the back of this workbook.

SOME EXAMPLES OF
COMPLETE MARRIAGE SERVICES

In this chapter you will find ten complete marriage services. The model for most of them is the traditional Episcopal service from the **Book of Common Prayer**. It is important to notice that all these services have the same basic understanding of Christian marriage. The basic difference between them is the kind of language used and the number of worship elements included. **Items set in boldface type are directions for the use of the service. This also includes certain abbreviations. M is for Minister, B for bride, G for groom, and L for lector.** Responses for the congregation are printed in capitals, as well as responses for the bride and groom, etc. Unless otherwise designated, material in lower case is spoken by the minister. Parts for a Lector are designated with an L. The lector may be another minister, a member of the wedding party, or someone designated by the couple.

THE TRADITIONAL EPISCOPAL SERVICE

Introductory Statement   **A1**
Dearly beloved, we are gathered together here in the sight of God, and in the face of this company, to join together this man and this woman in holy matrimony, which is an honorable estate, instituted of God, signifying unto us the mystical union that is betwixt Christ and his Church, which holy estate Christ adorned and beautified with his presence and first miracle that he wrought in Cana of Galilee, and is commended of Saint Paul to be honorable among all men, and therefore is not by any to be entered into unadvisedly or lightly, but reverently, discreetly, advisedly, soberly, and in the fear of God. Into this holy estate these two persons present come now to be joined. If any man can show just cause, why they may not lawfully be joined together, let him

now speak, or else hereafter forever hold his peace.
**The minister speaking unto the persons to be married
shall say:**

I require and charge you both, as ye will answer at
the dreadful day of judgment when the secrets of all
hearts shall be disclosed, that if either of you know any
impediment, why ye may not be lawfully joined together
in matrimony, ye do now confess it. For be ye well
assured that if any persons are joined together
otherwise than as God's Word doth allow, their marriage
is not lawful.

Declaration of Intent   **A2**

G..........wilt thou have this woman to thy wedded
wife, to live together after God's ordinance in the holy
estate of matrimony? Wilt thou love her, comfort her,
honor, and keep her in sickness and in health, and,
forsaking all others, keep thee only unto her, so long as
ye both shall life?
G I will

B..........wilt thou have this man to thy wedded
husband, to live together after God's ordinance in the
holy estate of matrimony? Wilt thou love him, comfort
him, honor, and keep him in sickness and in health, and,
forsaking all others, keep thee only unto him, so long as
ye both shall live?
B I will

Who giveth this woman to be married to this man?
The person giving the bride will respond
I do

Vows   **A3**
The man shall repeat

I..........take thee..........to my wedded wife, to have
and to hold from this day forward, for better or worse,
for richer for poorer, in sickness and in health, to love
and to cherish, till death us do part, according to God's
holy ordinance, and thereto I plight thee my troth.

The woman shall repeat

I..........take thee..........to my wedded husband, to have and to hold from this day forward, for better for worse, for richer for poorer, in sickness and in health, to love and to cherish, till death us do part, according to God's holy ordinance, and thereto I plight thee my troth.

Exchange of Rings A4

Before giving the ring to the man, the minister may say the following:

Bless, O Lord, this ring, that he who gives it and she who wears it may abide in thy peace, and continue in thy favor, unto their life's end; through Jesus Christ our Lord. Amen.

When placing the ring upon the woman's finger, the man shall say:

With this ring I thee wed, in the name of the Father, and of the Son, and of the Holy Ghost. Amen.

Prayers for the Marriage

Let us Pray

The minister and the people shall say the Lord's Prayer. Then the minister shall add:

O Eternal God, creator and preserver of all mankind, giver of all spiritual grace, the author of everlasting life, send thy blessing upon these thy servants, this man and this woman, whom we bless in thy name, that they, living faithfully together, may surely perform and keep the vow and covenant betwixt them made, whereof this ring given and received is a token and pledge, and may ever remain in perfect love and peace together, and live according to thy laws; through Jesus Christ our Lord. Amen. A5

The minister may add one or both of the following prayers.

O Almighty God, creator of mankind, who only art the well-spring of life, bestow upon these thy servants, if it be thy will, the gift and heritage of children, and grant that they may see their children brought up in thy faith and fear, to the honor and glory of thy name, through Jesus Christ our Lord. Amen. **A6**

O God, who hast so consecrated the state of matrimony that in it is represented the spiritual marriage and unity betwixt Christ and his Church, look mercifully upon these thy servants, that they may love, honor, and cherish each other, and so live together in faithfulness and patience, in wisdom and true godliness, that their home may be a haven of blessing and of peace, through the same Jesus Christ our Lord, who liveth and reigneth with thee and the Holy Spirit ever one God, world without end. Amen. **A7**

Declaration of Marriage **A8**
Then the minister shall join their right hands together and say:

Those whom God hath joined together let no man put asunder.

Forasmuch as .... and .... have consented together in holy wedlock, and have witnessed the same before God and this company, and thereto have given and pledged their troth, each to the other, and have declared the same by giving and receiving a ring, and by joining hands, I pronounce that they are man and wife, in the name of the Father, and the Son, and the Holy Ghost. Amen.

Benediction **A9**

God the Father, God the Son, God the Holy Ghost, bless, preserve, and keep you; the Lord mercifully with his favor look upon you, and fill you with all spiritual benediction and grace; that ye may so live together in this life, that in the world to come ye may have life everlasting. Amen.

[From the Book of Common Prayer.]

A CONTEMPORARY EPISCOPAL SERVICE

Introductory Statement   **B1**

Good people, we have come together in the presence of God to witness and proclaim the joining together of this man and this woman in marriage. The bond of marriage was established by God at creation, and our Lord Jesus Christ himself adorned this manner of life by his presence and first miracle at a wedding in Cana of Galilee. It signifies to us the union between Christ and his Church, and Holy Scripture commands it to be honored among all men.

The union of man and woman in heart, body, and mind is intended by God for their mutual joy; for the help and comfort given one another in prosperity and adversity; and, when it is God's will; for the procreation of children and their nuture in the knowledge and love of the Lord. Therefore marriage is not to be entered into unadvisedly or lightly, but reverently, deliberately, and in accord with the purposes for which it was instituted by God. Into this holy union..........and..........come now to be joined. If any of you can show just cause why they may not lawfully be married, speak now, or forever hold your peace.

Then the minister says to the persons to be married:

I require and charge you both in the name of God, that if either of you know any reason why you may not be united in marriage lawfully and in accordance with God's Word, you confess it now.

Declaration of Intent   **B2**

The minister then says to the man:

G..........will you have this woman to be your wife, to live together in a holy marriage? Will you love her, comfort her, honor and keep her, in sickness and in health, and forsaking all others, be faithful to her as long as you both shall life?

G I will by God's help

The minister then says to the woman:

B..........will you have this man to be your husband to live together in a holy marriage? Will you love him, comfort him, honor and keep him in sickness and in health, and forsaking all others, be faithful to him as long as you both shall live?

B I will by God's help

The minister addresses the following question to the wedding party and congregation:

Will you who witness these vows do all in your power to support and uphold this marriage in the years ahead?

We will

Who gives this woman to be married to this man?

The father or a friend says:

I do

The minister receives the woman at her father's or friend's hand and causes the man to take the woman's right hand in his.

Invocation   B3

The Lord be with you
    and also with you
Let us pray.

The people standing

Eternal God, creator and sustainer of all men, giver of all grace, author of salvation: Look with favor upon this man and this woman, that they may grow in love and peace together; through Jesus Christ your Son our Lord, who lives and reigns with you in the unity of the Holy Spriit, one God, now and forever, Amen.

Scripture Lessons   B4

Then one or more of the following passages from Holy Scripture is read. If there is to be a communion, a passage from the Gospels is always included.

The Lesson	The Gospel
Genesis 2:4-9, 15-24	Mark 10:6-9
Colossians 3:12-17	Matthew 7:21, 24-29

Ephesians 5:20-33   Matthew 5:13-16
1 Corinthians 13   John 15:11-17
1 John 4:7-16

Between the readings, Psalm 128, 113, or 100, or some other Psalm, Hymn, or Anthem may be sung or said. Homily

Vows   **B5**
All stand, and the man facing the woman, and taking her right hand in his, says:

I..........take you..........to be my wife, to have and to hold from this day forward, for better for worse, for richer for poorer, in sickness and in health, to love and to cherish, until we are parted by death. This is my solemn vow.

Then they loose their hands and the woman, still facing the man, takes his right hand in hers and says:

I..........take you..........to be my husband, to have and to hold from this day forward, for better for worse, for richer for poorer, in sickness and in health, to love and to cherish, until we are parted by death. This is my solemn vow.

Exchange of Rings   **B6**
The minister may ask God's blessing on the ring or rings, as follows:

Bless, O Lord, the ring that he who gives it and she who wears it may live in your peace, and continue in your favor, all the days of their life, through Jesus Christ our Lord. Amen.

The giver places the ring on the ring-finger of the other's hand, and says:

..........I give you this ring as a symbol of my vow, and with all that I am, and all that I have, I honor you in the name of God.

Declaration of Marriage   **B7**
Then the minister joins the right hands of the husband

and wife and says:

Now that..........and..........have given themselves to each other by solemn vows, with the joining of hands and the giving and receiving of a ring (rings), I pronounce that they are husband and wife, in the name of the Father, and of the Son, and of the Holy Spirit.

Those whom God has joined together let not man put asunder.

Amen.

Prayers for the Marriage

Let us pray together in the words our Savior taught us:

The Lord's Prayer
The minister says this prayer over the couple:

Almighty God, look graciously, we pray, on this man and this woman, and on all whom you make to be one flesh in holy marriage. Make their lives together a sacrament of your love to this broken world, so that unity may overcome estrangement, forgiveness heal guilt, and joy triumph over despair; in the name of our Lord Jesus Christ, to whom be all honor and glory, now and forever. Amen. **B8**

The minister then may add one or more of the following three prayers:

Almighty God, creator of mankind, the source of all life, grant to..........and........., if it be your will, the gift and heritage of children, and the grace to nurture them in the knowledge and love of your name; through Jesus Christ our Lord. Amen. **B9**

Almighty God, giver of life and love, bless..........and..........whom you have joined in holy matrimony. Grant them wisdom and devotion in the ordering of their common life that each may be to the other a strength in need, a counsellor in perplexity, a comfort in sorrow, and a companion in joy. And so knit their wills together in your will, and their spirits in your spirit, that they may live together in love and peace all the days of their life, through Jesus Christ our Lord. Amen.   **B10**

Almighty God, by whose love the whole world is created, sustained and redeemed, so fill.......... and .... with the overflowing abundance of your grace that their lives may reflect your compassion for all men. May their love for each other not blind them to the brokenness in the world. As you teach them to bind up each other's wounds, teach them also to heal the hurts of others. As their mutual respect orders their common life within the family, direct them to their share also in the shaping of a society in which human dignity may flourish and abound. At all times and in all seasons may they rejoice to serve you and to give you thanks, through Jesus Christ our Lord. Amen.   **B11**

The following prayer is always added, the couple kneeling:

O God, who consecrated the state of marriage to be a sign of the spiritual unity between Christ and his Church: Bless these your servants, that they may love, honor, and cherish each other in faithfulness and patience, in wisdom and true godliness, and that their home may be a haven of blessing and peace; through Jesus Christ our Lord, who lives and reigns with you and the Holy Spirit, one God, now and forever. Amen.   **15E**

Benediction   **B13**

God the Father, God the Son, God the Holy Spirit, bless, preserve and keep you; the Lord mercifully with his favor look upon you and fill you with all spiritual benediction and grace, that you may faithfully live together in this life, and in the world to come have life everlasting. Amen.

(From **Services For Trial Use,** © 1971, The Church Hymnal Corporation. Used by permission.)

THE UNITED METHODIST SERVICE

Introductory Statement C1

Dearly beloved, we are gathered together here in the sight of God, and in the presence of these witnesses, to join together .... and .... in holy matrimony; which is an honorable estate, instituted of God, and signifying unto us the mystical union which exists between Christ and his Church; which holy estate Christ adorned and beautified with his presence in Cana of Galilee. It is therefore not to be entered into unadvisedly, but reverently, discreetly, and in the fear of God. Into this holy estate these two persons come now to be joined. If any man can show just cause why they may not lawfully be joined together, let him now speak, or else hereafter forever hold his peace.

Addressing the persons to be married, the minister shall say:

I require and charge you both, as you stand in the presence of God, before whom the secrets of all hearts are disclosed, that, having duly considered the holy covenant you are about to make, you do now declare before this company your pledge of faith, each to the other. Be well assured that if these solemn vows are kept inviolate, as God's Word demands, and if steadfastly you endeavor to do the will of your heavenly Father, God will bless your marriage, will grant you fulfillment in it, and will establish your home in peace.

Declaration of Intent C2

G.......... wilt thou have this woman to be thy wedded wife, to live together in the holy estate of matrimony? Wilt thou love her, comfort her, honor and keep her, in sickness and in health; and forsaking all others keep thee only unto her so long as ye both shall live?

G I will

B.......... wilt thou have this man to be thy wedded husband, to live together in the holy estate of matrimony? Wilt thou love him, comfort him, honor and keep him, in sickness and in health; and forsaking all others keep thee only unto him so long as ye both shall live?

B I will

Who giveth this woman to be married to this man?
The father of the woman, or whoever gives her in marriage shall answer:

I do

Vows   C3

I .... take thee .... to be my wedded wife, to have and to hold, from this day forward, for better, for worse, for richer, for poorer, in sickness and in health, to love and to cherish, till death us do part, according to God's holy ordinance; and thereto I pledge thee my faith.

I .... take thee .... to be my wedded husband, to have and to hold, from this day forward, for better, for worse, for richer, for poorer, in sickness and in health, to love and to cherish, till death us do part, according to God's holy ordinance; and thereto I pledge thee my faith.

Exchange of Rings   C4
The minister taking the ring or rings shall say:

The wedding ring is the outward and visible sign of an inward and spiritual grace, signifying to all the uniting of this man and woman in holy matrimony, through the Church of Jesus Christ our Lord.

Let us Pray.

Bless, O Lord, the giving of these rings, that they who wear them may abide in thy peace, and continue in thy favor; through Jesus Christ our Lord. Amen.

If there be but one ring the minister may say:

Bless, O Lord, the giving of this ring, that he who gives it and she who wears it may abide forever in thy peace, and continue in thy favor; through Jesus Christ our Lord. Amen.

In giving the ring the man and the woman shall say:

In token and pledge of our constant faith and abiding love, with this ring I thee wed, in the name of the Father, and of the Son, and of the Holy Spirit. Amen.

Declaration of Marriage C5

Forasmuch as .... and .... have consented together in holy wedlock, and have witnessed the same before God and this company and thereto have pledged their faith each to the other, and have declared the same by joining hands and by giving and receiving rings; I pronounce that they are husband and wife together, in the name of the Father, and of the Son, and of the Holy Spirit. Those whom God hath joined together, let not man put asunder. Amen.

Prayers for the Marriage C6

Let us Pray.

O eternal God, creator and preserver of all mankind, giver of all spiritual grace, the author of everlasting life: send thy blessing upon this man and this woman, whom we bless in thy name; that they may surely perform and keep the vow and covenant between them made, and may ever remain in perfect love and peace together, and live according to thy laws.

Look graciously upon them, that they may love, honor, and cherish each other, and so live together in faithfulness and patience, in wisdom and true godliness, that their home may be a haven of blessing and a place of peace, through Jesus Christ our Lord. Amen.

The people and the minister shall say the Lord's Prayer.

Benediction C7

God the Father, the Son, and the Holy Spirit bless, preserve, and keep you; the Lord graciously with his favor look upon you, and so fill you with life that in the world to come you may have life everlasting. Amen.

THE TRADITIONAL PRESBYTERIAN SERVICE

Introductory Statement   **D1**

Dearly beloved, we are assembled here in the presence of God, to join this man and this woman in holy marriage, which is instituted by God, regulated by his commandments, blessed by our Lord Jesus Christ, and to be held in honor among all men. Let us reverently remember that God has established and sanctified marriage, for the welfare and happiness of mankind. Our Savior has declared that a man shall leave his father and mother and cleave unto his wife. By his apostles, he has instructed those who enter this relationship to cherish a mutual esteem and love; to bear with each other's infirmities and weaknesses; to comfort each other in sickness, trouble, and sorrow; to provide for each other, and for their household, in temporal things; to pray for and encourage each other in the things which pertain to God; and to live together as heirs of the grace of life. **Then speaking to the persons who are to be married, the minister shall say:**

I charge you both before God, the searcher of hearts, that if you know any reason why you may not be joined in marriage, you say so; for God is a God of truth.

Invocation   **D2**

Let us Pray.

Almighty and ever-blessed God, whose presence is the happiness of every condition, and whose favor hallows every relation, we beseech thee to be present and favorable unto these thy servants, that they may be truly joined in the honorable estate of marriage, and in covenant with thee, O God. As thou has brought them together by thy providence, sanctify them by thy Spirit, giving them a new frame of heart fit for their new estate; and enrich them with all grace, whereby they may enjoy the comforts, undergo the cares, endure the trials, and perform the duties of life together as Christians, under thy heavenly guidance and protection, through our Lord Jesus Christ. Amen.

Declaration of Intent   D3

G . . . . wilt thou have this woman to be thy wife, and wilt thou pledge thy troth to her, in all love and honor, in all duty and service, in all faith and tenderness, to live with her, and cherish her, according to the ordinance of God, in the holy bond of marriage?

G I will

B . . . . wilt thou have this man to be thy husband, and wilt thou pledge thy troth to him in all love and honor, in all duty and service, in all faith and tenderness, to live with him, and cherish him, according to the ordinance of God, in the holy bond of marriage?

B I will

Who giveth this woman to be married to this man? **Then the father, or guardian, or friend of the woman shall say:**

I do.

Vows   D4

I . . . . take thee . . . . to be my wedded wife; and I do promise and covenant, before God and these witnesses, to be thy loving and faithful husband, in plenty and in want, in joy and in sorrow, in sickness and in health, as long as we both shall live.

I . . . . take thee . . . . to be my wedded husband; and I do promise and covenant, before God and these witnesses, to be thy loving and faithful wife, in plenty and in want, in joy and in sorrow, in sickness and in health, as long as we both shall live.

Exchange of Rings   D5
Before the giving of the ring the minister may say:

Bless, O Lord, this ring, that he/she who gives it and she/he who wears it may abide in thy peace, and continue in thy favor, unto their life's end, through Jesus Christ our Lord. Amen.

The man/woman shall give the ring saying:

This ring I give thee in token and pledge, of our constant faith and abiding love.

or

With this ring I thee wed, in the name of the Father, and of the Son, and of the Holy Spirit. Amen.

Prayers for the Marriage   D6

Let us Pray.

Most merciful and gracious God, of whom the whole family in heaven and earth is named, bestow upon these thy servants the seal of thine approval, and thy fatherly benediction, granting unto them grace to fulfill, with pure and steadfast affection, the vow and covenant between them made. Guide them together, we beseech thee, in the way of righteousness and peace, that, loving and serving thee, with one heart and mind, all the days of their life, they may be abundantly enriched with the tokens of thy everlasting favor, in Jesus Christ our Lord. Amen.

Then let all pray together the Lord's Prayer

Declaration of Marriage   D7

By the authroity committed unto me as a minister of the Church of Christ, I declare that .... and .... are now husband and wife according to the ordinance of God, and the law of the state, in the name of the Father, and of the Son, and of the Holy Spirit. Amen.

Whom therefore God has joined together, let no man put asunder.

Benediction D8

The Lord bless you and keep you, the Lord make his face to shine upon you and be gracious unto you, the Lord lift up his countenance upon you and give you peace. Amen.

(From **The Book of Common Worship**, © 1946, by the Board of Christian Education of the Presbyterian Church in the United States of America. Used by permission.)

A CONTEMPORARY PRESBYTERIAN SERVICE

Call to Worship E1

Let us worship God.

There was a marriage at Cana in Galilee. Jesus was invited to the marriage with his disciples.

Introductory Statement E2

Friends, marriage is established by God. In marriage a man and a woman willingly bind themselves together in love and become one even as Christ is one with the church, his body.

Let marriage be held in honor among all.

All may join in a hymn of praise and the following prayer.

Prayer of Confession E3

Let us confess our sin before God.

Almighty God, our Father, you created us for life together. We confess that we have turned from your will. We have not loved one another as you commanded. We have been quick to claim our own rights and careless of the rights of others. We have taken much and given little. Forgive our disobedience, O God, and strengthen us in love, so that we may serve you as a faithful people, and live together in your joy, through Jesus Christ our Lord. Amen.

Declaration of Pardon E4
Hear and believe the good news of the gospel. Nothing can separate us from the love of God in Christ Jesus our Lord.

In Jesus we are forgiven.

The people may stand to sing a doxology, or some other appropriate response to the mercy of God. The minister or lector may offer a prayer for illumination before reading the Old Testament lesson.

Scripture Lessons
The lesson is .... listen for the Word of God.

The Gloria Patri or some other response may be sung.
The lesson is .... listen for the Word of God.

Homily

Vows E5
Then let the minister address the man and woman saying:
.... and .... you have come together according to God's wonderful plan for creation. Now, before these people say your vows to each other.

Let the man and the woman stand before the people facing each other. Then the minister shall say:
Be subject to one another out of reverence for Christ.

The man shall say to the woman:
.... I promise with God's help to be your faithful husband, to love and serve you as Christ commands, as long as we both shall live.

The woman shall say to the man:
.... I promise with God's help to be your faithful wife, to love and serve you as Christ commands, as long as we both shall live.

Exchange of Rings E6
A ring, or rings, may be given with the following words:
I give you this ring as a sign of my promise.

The minister shall then say:

As God's picked representatives of the new humanity, purified and beloved of God himself, be merciful in action, kindly in heart, humble in mind. Accept life, and be most patient and tolerant with one another. Forgive as freely as the Lord has forgiven you. And, above everything else, be truly loving. Let the peace of Christ rule in your hearts, remembering that as members of the one body you are called to live in harmony, and never forget to be thankful for what God has done for you.

or

Love is slow to lose patience, it looks for a way of being constructive. It is not possessive. It is neither anxious to impress nor does it cherish inflated ideas of its own importance. Love has good manners and does not pursue selfish advantage. It is not touchy. It does not keep account of evil or gloat over the wickedness of other people. On the contrary, it is glad with all good men when truth prevails. Love knows no limit to its endurance, no end to its trust, no fading of its hope. It can outlast anything. It still stands when all else has fallen.

Prayers for the Marriage   **E7**

Praise the Lord
The Lord's name be praised
Lift up your hearts
We lift them to the Lord.
Let us pray.

Eternal God, without your grace no promise is sure. Strengthen .... and .... with the gift of your Spirit, so they may fulfill the vows they have taken. Keep them faithful to each other and to you. Fill them with such love and joy that they may build a home where no one is a stranger. And guide them by your word to serve you all the days of their lives, through Jesus Christ our Lord, to whom be honor and glory forever and ever. Amen.

The Lord's Prayer shall be said.

Declaration of Marriage E8
.... and .... you are now husband and wife according to the witness of the Holy Catholic Church, and the law of the state. Become one. Fulfill your promises. Love and serve the Lord.
What God has united, man must not divide.

Benediction E9
Glory be to him who can keep you from falling and bring you safe to his glorious presence, innocent and happy. To God, the only God, who saves us through Jesus Christ our Lord, be the glory, majesty, authority, and power, which he had before time began, now and forever. Amen.
or
The grace of the Lord Jesus Christ, the love of God, and the fellowship of the Holy Spirit, be with you all. Amen. E10
(From **The Worship Book,** © MCMLXX, MCMLXXII, The Westminster Press. Used by permission.)

THE TRADITIONAL LUTHERAN SERVICE

When a marriage is solemnized in the Church, a Hymn may be sung, and Psalm 67 or Psalm 128 may be sung or said, ending with the Gloria Patri. If there be an address (homily) it may then follow.

Invocation

Introductory Statement F1
In the name of the Father, and of the Son, and of the Holy Ghost. Amen.
Dearly beloved, forasmuch as marriage is a holy

estate, ordained of God, and to be held in honor by all, it becometh those who enter therein to weigh, with reverent minds, what the Word of God teacheth concerning it.

The Lord God said: It is not good that the man should be alone; I will make him a help meet for him.

Our Lord Jesus Christ said: Have ye not read that he which made them at the beginning made them male and female, and said, For this cause shall a man leave his father and mother, and shall cleave to his wife, and they twain shall be one flesh? Wherefore, they are no more twain, but one flesh. What therefore God hath joined together, let no man put asunder.

Scripture Lessons   F2
Then shall be read one or both of the following Lections:
The Apostle Paul, speaking by the Holy Spirit saith: "Husbands, love your wives, even as Christ also loved the Church, and gave himself for it. He that loveth his wife, loveth himself; for no man ever yet hated his own flesh, but nourisheth it, even as the Lord the Church. Wives, submit yourselves unto your own husbands as unto the Lord; for the husband is the head of the wife, even as Christ is the head of the Church."
and, or
The Apostle Peter, speaking by the Holy Spirit, saith: "Ye wives, let your adorning be the ornament of a meek and quiet spirit, which is, in the sight of God, of great price. Likewise, ye husbands, dwell with them according to knowledge, giving honor unto the wife as unto the weaker vessel and as being heirs together of the grace of life."

And although, by reason of sin, many a cross hath been laid thereon, nevertheless our gracious Father in heaven doth not forsake his children in an estate so holy and acceptable to him, but is ever present with his abundant blessing.

Declaration of Intent   **F3**

Into this holy estate this man and this woman come now to be united. If any one, therefore, can show just cause why they may not be lawfully joined together, let him now speak, or else forever hold his peace.

Then the minister shall say to the man and the woman:

G .... wilt thou have this woman to thy wedded wife, to live together after God's ordinance in the holy estate of matrimony? Wilt thou love her, comfort her, honor and keep her in sickness and in health, and, forsaking all others, keep thee only unto her, so long as ye both shall live?

G I will

B .... wilt thou have this man to thy wedded husband, to live together after God's ordinance in the holy estate of matrimony? Wilt thou love him, comfort him, honor and keep him in sickness and in health, and, forsaking all others, keep thee only unto him, so long as ye both shall live?

B I will

Who giveth this woman to be married to this man?

The father or friend of the woman will say:

I do.

Vows   **F4**

The man shall take the right hand of the woman and say after the minister:

I .... take thee .... to be my wedded wife, to have and to hold from this day forward, for better for worse, for richer for poorer, in sickness and in health, to love and to cherish, till death us do part, according to God's holy ordinance, and thereto I plight thee my troth.

Then shall the woman in like manner say after the minister:

I .... take thee .... to be my wedded husband, to have and to hold from this day forward, for better for worse, for richer for poorer, in sickness and in health, to love and to cherish, till death us do part, according to God's holy ordinance, and thereto I plight thee my troth.

Vows F5
Should a shorter form be desired, the following may be said by the man:
> I .... take thee .... to my wedded wife, and plight thee my troth, till death us do part.

The following, in like manner, may be said by the woman:
> I .... take thee .... to my wedded husband, and plight thee my troth, till death us do part.

Exchange of Rings F6
In giving the ring the man and the woman shall say:
> Receive this ring as a token of wedded love and troth.

Declaration of Marriage F7
Then the minister shall say:
> Join your right hands.

Then shall the minister lay his right hand upon their hands and say:
> Forasmuch as .... and .... have consented together in holy wedlock, and have declared the same before God and in the presence of this company, I pronounce them man and wife, in the name of the Father and of the Son and of the Holy Ghost. Amen.

> What God hath joined together, let not man put asunder.

Prayers for the Marriage
Then they may kneel, and the minister shall bless them saying:
> The Lord God, who created our first parents and sanctified their union in marriage, sanctify and bless you, that ye may please him both in body and soul, and live together in holy love until life's end. Amen.

Then the minister shall say:
> Let us pray.

> Almighty and most merciful God, who hast now united this man and this woman in the holy estate of

matrimony, grant them grace to live therein according to thy holy Word. Strengthen them in constant fidelity and true affection toward each other. Sustain and defend them amidst all trials and temptations, and help them so to pass through this world in faith toward thee, in communion with thy holy Church, and in loving service one of the other, that they may enjoy forever thy heavenly benediction, through Jesus Christ, thy Son our Lord, who liveth and reigneth with thee and the Holy Ghost, one God, world without end. Amen.   **F8**

The minister may add one or both of the following prayers:

O almighty God, creator of mankind, who only art the wellspring of life, bestow upon these thy servants, if it be thy will, the gift and heritage of children, and grant that they may see their children brought up in thy faith and fear, to the honor and glory of thy name, through Jesus Christ our Lord. Amen.   **F9**

or

O God, who art our dwelling place in all generations, look with favor upon the homes of our land. Enfold husbands and wives, parents and children, in the bonds of thy pure love, and so bless our homes, that they may be a shelter for the defenseless, a bulwark for the tempted, a resting place for the weary, and a foretaste of our eternal home in thee, through Jesus Christ our Lord. Amen.   **F10**

Then shall all say the Lord's Prayer

Benediction   **F11**

The Lord bless thee and keep thee. The Lord make his face to shine upon thee, and be gracious unto thee. The Lord lift up his countenance upon thee, and give thee peace. Amen.

or

God Almighty send you his light and truth to keep you all the days of your life. The hand of God protect you; his holy angels accompany you. God the Father, God the

Son, and God the Holy Ghost, cause his grace to be
mighty upon you. Amen. **F12**
(From **The Lutheran Service Book and Hymnal,** by
permission of The Commission on the Liturgy and
Hymnal.)

A CONTEMPORARY SERVICE BASED ON THE LUTHERAN TRADITION

**When a marriage is to be held in a church building a
hymn may be sung, and Psalm 67, or Psalm 128, may be
sung or said, ending with the Gloria Patri. A Scripture
lesson may be read by a lector or member of the wedding
party, and a homily by the minister may follow.**

Invocation **G1**
In the name of the Father, the Son, and the Holy
Spirit. Amen.
Let us pray:
Eternal God, in your love and divine wisdom you
have created us male and female so that we may be
joined in marriage and know the love and joy you have
prepared for us. We pray that you will be present and
look with favor upon .... and .... your servants
who now come before you to be joined as husband and
wife. Send your Spirit upon them that they may know
the joy of your guiding presence through all the days of
their life together. Amen.

Introductory Statement **G2**
Friends, God in his love and goodness toward us has
given us marriage to be a precious gift. Through this gift
we can know the deepest human relationship, one which
almost touches heaven itself. It is through this precious
gift that God raises up for himself new life, to be children
of the covenant, praising his name and making visible his
holy will.

God has created us male and female to walk together, side by side. In marriage two individuals become one flesh, united in love, in purpose, and in spirit. As our Lord taught us, "From the beginning of creation God made them male and female. For this reason a man shall leave his father and mother and be joined to his wife, and the two shall become one. So they are no longer two but one. What therefore God has joined together, let not man put asunder." *TEAR APART*

Marriage is sacred and holy, and it requires more of two individuals than they in their own strength can offer. God in his infinite mercy knows our weakness and has given us his Spirit to guide us and empower us so that we can be what he calls us to be.

.... and .... if you will rely upon the power and promise God gives us, and you will know a deeper love, a more vital relationship, and a harmony of life which will lead you through all the trials and adversities you may face.

Declaration of Intent   G3

The minister will address first the man, then the woman, and finally the parents of both.

.... do you desire to be united in marriage with .... , and will you love her, comfort her, honor her, and be her helper as long as you both shall live?

I do and I will.

.... do you desire to be united in marriage with .... and will you love him, comfort him, honor him, and be his helper as long as you both shall live?

I do and I will.

The parents of the bride and groom will stand.

Will you the parents of .... and .... do all in your power to uphold their marriage in the years ahead, and will you promise to pray for and encourage them that they may fulfill the vows they are making today?

We will.

Vows   **G4**
**The wedding party will proceed to the altar where the
bride and groom shall face each other and join hands.**
.... and .... you are now about to commit yourselves to each other in the bonds of Christian marriage.
This is the most solemn moment in a marriage service,
for here you make your promises to God and to each
other.

G .... I promise before God, our family, and
friends to be your loving and faithful husband, to share
my life with you, in wealth and in poverty, in sickness
and in health, in good times and in bad times for as long
as we both shall live.

B .... I promise before God, our family, and friends
to be your loving and faithful wife, to share my life with
you, in wealth and in poverty, in sickness and in health,
in good times and in bad times for as long as we both
shall live.

Exchange of Rings   **G5**
The man and the woman may exchange rings and say:
This ring is a symbol of my love and faithfulness.

Declaration of Marriage   **G6**
**The minister shall have the man and woman join hands,
and then he shall lay his hand upon their hands and say:**
.... and .... you have now been joined together
in Christian marriage, and I now declare that you are
husband and wife according to the witness of the
Christian Church and the laws of the state. In the name
of the Father, the Son, and the Holy Spirit. Amen.

Prayers for the Marriage
**The couple may kneel and receive the blessing of the
pastor and parents.**
The Lord God, the creator of the heavens and the
earth, who gave life to our first parents and blessed their
marriage, bless you that you may grow together in holy

love and spend the days of your life praising and glorifying him who loved us and gave himself for us. Amen. **G7**

The parents standing behind the couple may say:

May God's Spirit be upon you to guide and sustain you, and give you love beyond measure.

The couple stands. The minister, a lector, or one of the wedding party may offer the biddings for the following prayers.

L Let us give thanks to God for his gifts and his goodness to us today.

All may pray silently.

M Lord God, we give you praise and thanksgiving for all your gifts. We thank you that you created us, gave us the breath of life, and the ability to be one with another in faithfulness and in love. We thank you for the love that has been formed in the hearts of .... and .... Let your hand be upon them so that their love will grow and bloom as a flower in your kingdom. Amen. **G8**

L Let us pray for .... and ....

All may pray silently.

M Father of love and mercy, pour out your grace upon .... and .... and give them the power of your Spirit, so that they may fulfill with pure hearts and steady faith the vows made here today. Grant them courage for times of testing, endurance for times of trial, strength for times of weakness, but above all a constant love to knit together the heights and depths they will know. Lead them to that joy which only comes through your divine presence in all of life. Amen. **G9**

L Let us pray for all the families of the earth.

All may pray silently.

M Eternal God, in your wisdom you have given us families for our refuge and strength here on earth. We pray for all the families of the earth, and especially those families gathered here today. Remind us of the bonds which unite us and the high goals you set before us. Deliver us from every evil which will tear us apart, and strengthen every good impulse that our family life will

be stronger, and that children will know a foretaste of your love and devotion, through the shared love and faith of a mother and a father. These prayers we ask in the name of Jesus Christ our Lord. Amen. **G10**
All present will join in the Lord's Prayer.

Benediction — *YES* **G11**
May the blessings of God almighty be with you. Amen.
May he give you his peace. Amen.
May God the Father, the Son, and the Holy Spirit keep you and sustain you all the days of your life. Amen.

KISS?

A CONTEMPORARY SERVICE BASED ON THE PRESBYTERIAN TRADITION

Call to Worship **H1**
Our Lord Jesus said: from the beginning of creation, God made them male and female. For this reason a man shall leave his father and mother and be joined to his wife, so they are no longer two but one.
Let us worship God.

Hymn

Invocation **H2**
Let us pray.
Almighty God, whose presence is the happiness of every condition, and whose favor makes all our relationships holy, we ask you to be present and to look with favor upon .... and .... , that they may be joined in Christian marriage, as they make their promises in your presence.
Eternal God, since you are our creator and give us the very breath of life, we ask you to guide these two in their life together. Give them a spirit of love and faithfulness, which will allow them to share the love, undergo

the cares, endure the trials, and perform the duties of life together as Christians, under your divine guidance and protection, through Jesus Christ our Lord. Amen.

Scripture Lesson

Hear the Word of God as it is written in .... the .... chapter, verses ....

Let these words guide all of us in our homes and marriages.

Introductory Statement   H3

Friends. we are gathered here in the presence of God to join .... and .... in holy marriage. For Christians, marriage is instituted of God, and it is holy. Marriage is to be regulated by his commandments, for through them we live as we were created to live. Marriage is blessed by our Lord Jesus Christ, and we believe that it is to be held in honor by all men.

God, our Heavenly Father has established marriage for our welfare and our happiness. Through Jesus Christ we are told that a man shall leave his father and mother and live as one with his wife. Through the teachings of the apostles, Jesus has instructed those who marry to love each other, to be patient and kind with each other's problems and weaknesses, to comfort each other in sorrow and sickness, to provide for each other and for their children the things which pertain to earthly life, and to pray for and encourage each other in the worship and service of God, and in those things which are eternal.

.... and .... if you will do these things you will know love and joy, and eternal happiness. Amen.

Declaration of Intent   H4

.... will you take .... to be your wife, and will you be faithful to her, to love her, to honor her, to live with her and cherish her according to the commandments of God in holy marriage?

G I will.

.... will you take .... to be your husband, and will you be faithful to him, to love him, to honor him, to live with him and cherish him according to the commandments of God in holy marraige?

B I will.

Who gives this woman to be married to this man?

The father or friend of the woman responds:

I do.

Vows H5

.... I promise before God and these witnesses to be your loving and faithful husband, in joy and sorrow, through sickness and health, in times of plenty or want, as long as we both shall live.

.... I promise before God and these witnesses to be your loving and faithful wife, in joy and sorrow, through sickness and health, in times of plenty or want, as long as we both shall live.

Exchange of Rings H6

The minister shall take the rings into his hand and shall offer this prayer:

Let us pray.

Eternal God, we pray for your blessings upon these rings that they may be a permanent reminder of holy promises and steadfast love. Bless these who wear them that they may remain in your favor throughout all their earthly life, through Jesus Christ our Lord. Amen.

Let the man and woman exchange rings and say:

This ring is the sign of my promise, and I give it to you in the name of the Father, and of the Son, and of the Holy Spirit. Amen.

Prayers for the Marriage H7

Let us pray.

Eternal God, we ask you to give your divine approval and blessing to .... and .... We pray that they will find through your grace, the power to fulfill their vows,

and live together in love and harmony all the days of
their life. Guide them through the difficult times, and
give them a love that will deepen day by day, and year
by year. May faith and holiness be the results of their
marriage, that your name and presence will be felt in
their home, helping them, guiding their children, and
making the way to life eternal, through Jesus Christ our
Lord. Amen.

Hear us now as we pray the prayer Jesus taught us
saying, Our Father . . . Amen.

Declaration of Marriage   H8

I now declare that .... and .... are husband
and wife, according to the witness of the Christian
Church, and the laws of the state, in the name of the
Father, and of the Son, and the Holy Spirit. Amen.

What therefore God has joined together, let not man
put asunder.

Benediction   H9

The Lord bless you and keep you, the Lord make his
face to shine upon you, and be gracious to you, the Lord
lift up his face upon you and give you peace, both now
and forevermore. Amen.

A CONTEMPORARY
NON-DENOMINATIONAL SERVICE

This service emphasizes the personal and biblical aspects
of marriage. It stresses marriage as a part of the worship
of the church. The minister enters the sanctuary before
the wedding party at the conclusion of the Prelude.

Call to Worship   I1

We are gathered here to worship God and to witness
the marriage vows of .... and .... (full names). Let
your light so shine before men that they may see your

good works and give glory to your Father who is in heaven.

Let us worship God.

Hymn
During this hymn the wedding party enters the church.

Prayers of Invocation and Confession   **12**

We do not come to God offering our perfection. We come to him humbly, offering ourselves, in all our imperfection. Let us pray to God for mercy and forgiveness, that we too may learn to offer each other forgiveness as we have been forgiven.

Eternal God, we do not presume to offer anything to you that is worthy of your love and righteousness. We offer ourselves, in all our imperfection, in our sins and our selfishness. Forgive us, Father, and help us to forgive one another as you forgive us.

At this joyous time, help us to commit ourselves to the meaning and the mystery of marriage. Help us to stand with .... and .... as they begin a new relationship under your divine guidance. Lead us all to practice the love and forgiveness which will strengthen this marriage, through Jesus Christ our Lord. Amen.

Declaration of Pardon   **13**

Jesus Christ has died for our sins, and in him, God grants us forgiveness. Believe this good news, accept his forgiveness, and turn to serve him. Make his way your life. Amen.

Scripture Lessons

In holy Scripture God has given us a divine guide for life and for the marriages we establish in his name. Let us read from his holy Word.

It would be appropriate to have a member of the wedding party read one of the Scripture lessons.

The Old Testament lesson is

58

This is God's Word and it is for us.

The Old Testament lesson may be followed by a response. The response may be a psalm, or an instrumental or vocal solo. Psalms 100 would be a good selection.

The New Testament lesson is ....

This is God's Word and it will lead us to eternal life.

Introductory Statement   14

.... and .... you are entering into a new experience and a holy relationship. "It is a chief moment in life when two people, who were strangers to one another, are drawn together by an irresistible attraction, so that their souls cannot be henceforth divided by time or space; when one sees in a single woman that dream of purity and sweetness which has ever haunted his soul; when in a single man she finds the rest and satisfaction her heart has been unconsciously seeking. It is a revelation from above, and makes all things new; it is the hand of Providence, and annuls every argument of worldly providence."

You are performing an act of utter faith, believing in one another to the end.

As the bride gives herself to the bridegroom, let him be to her now father and mother, sister and brother, and most sacred — husband. As he gives himself to her, let the bride sustain and inspire his heart in the great affairs of life and in his chosen calling.

If you wish your new estate to be touched with perennial beauty, cherish those gracious visions which have made spring within your hearts during the days of your betrothal. You must never forget or deny the vision you once saw; you must resolve that it be not blotted out nor blurred by the commonplace experiences of life. Faults may appear which were once hidden in a golden mist; excellencies may seem to fade in the glare of the noonday sun. Still be unmoved in your devotion; still remain confident and hopeful. Amid the reality of present imperfection, believe in the ideal. You saw it once. It still exists. It is the final truth.

This is the man, that is the woman you love. That is the shape of spiritual beauty God sees and which for an hour he showed to you. That is the soul which is to be when this conflict with temptations, hindrances, failures is accomplished. Hide that imagination in your inmost heart. Make real this ideal in your united lives and your home will be a "place of repair and harbor," a dwelling place of contentment and abiding joy, a foretaste of that heavenly habitation where goodness reigns and love is the very air, the kingdom and home of our Father above. Amen.

This address is taken from KATE CARNEGIE by Ian Maclaren.

Declaration of Intent I5

Christian marriage is most serious, because it will bind you together for life in a relationship so close and so intimate that the two of you will become one. Before you lies a future with its hopes and disappointments, its successes and its failures, its pleasures and its pains, its joy and its sorrows. These elements are mingled in every life and are to be expected. But for Christians they are not there to be received with resignation, but with hope and joy and all the spiritual gifts God's Spirit promises us.

G .... do you come here freely to take .... as your wife, according to the commandments of God in holy marriage?

G I do.

B .... do you come here freely to take .... as your husband, according to the commandments of God in holy marriage?

B I do.

The parents of the man and woman will stand. The father or friend of the woman may give her hand to the man at this time.

Do you the parents of .... and .... promise that you will encourage them with your example and your prayers that their marriage will be strong and endure. **The parents will say:**
We do.

Hymn or Solo

Vows   16
Since you have chosen to enter into marriage, join your right hands and declare your marriage vows here before God and these people.
G I .... take you .... to be my wife and I promise before God and these friends that I will share my life with you in all love and honor, in all faith and tenderness, through joy and sorrow, in sickness and health, as long as we both shall live.
B I .... take you .... to be my husband and I promise before God and these friends that I will share my life with you in all love and honor, in all faith and tenderness, through joy and sorrow, in sickness and health, as long as we both shall live.

Exchange of Rings   17
The minister shall receive both rings and will offer this prayer:
Let us pray.
Eternal God, bless these rings that as .... and .... wear them they will be reminded of their faith in you and their promises to each other. Let these rings be symbols of a deep faith and an unending love, through Jesus Christ our Lord. Amen.
In giving the rings let the man and the woman say:
.... this ring is the sign of my love and faithfulness, and I give it to you in the name of the Father, the Son, and the Holy Spirit. Amen.

Declaration of Marriage · I8

Since you have made holy promises to God and to each other, I declare that you are now husband and wife according to the witness of the Christian Church and the law of the state, in the name of the Father, the Son, and the Holy Spirit. Amen.

Whom God has joined together, let not man put asunder.

Prayers for the Marriage

Let us pray.

M Eternal God, we thank you for life, its wonder and mystery. We thank you for the capacity to share love with one another, and know the joys of that gift you gave us, when you created us in your own image. Father, we pray now for .... and .... that your hand will be upon them, guiding them and leading them through their married life together. Grant them your blessing and your Spirit so that as they walk through the daylight and darkness of life, they may know that strength which only comes from your divine presence. **I9**

G Eternal God, help me to be a Christian man and a loving husband. Make firm in my life the vows of marriage, that I may walk in your will and be the person you would have me be. **I10**

B Heavenly Father, guide me and help me to be the Christian person you would have me be, so that I will be a loving wife in the years ahead. So bless our home that all will know that you are our heavenly Father. **I11**

M For these prayers and intentions we ask your divine benediction. Help us all to make our lives true temples of your Spirit. We pray your blessing upon every home which has led to the founding of this new marriage. May we all stand under your love and direction that we will help .... and .... to know the joy and wonder of life within your divine purposes through Jesus Christ our Lord. Amen. **I12**

The prayers will conclude with the Lord's Prayer.

Benediction 113

Now to him who by the power at work within us is able to do far more abundantly than all that we ask or think, to him be glory in the Church and in Christ Jesus to all generations, forever and ever. Amen.

Hymn
During this hymn the wedding party and the ministers will leave the sanctuary.

A ROMAN CATHOLIC SERVICE

The following is the rite for celebrating marriage outside Mass. Normally the celebration of marriage in the Roman Catholic Church takes place during Mass. However, when there is a good reason the following marriage rite can be used outside Mass, see note 13, page 63. For the purposes of this book the Marriage Rite without Mass is used here, and should be of interest to couples who are planning a marriage where one of the partners is Roman Catholic and the other partner is from some other Christian Church.

The text of the Roman Rite uses slightly different headings for the parts of the marriage service, than are mentioned for the other services in this book. The following headings and numbers may help you compare the various parts. The Rite begins with a SERVICE OF THE WORD, nos. 40-42. The Marriage Rite itself has an INTRODUCTION, no. 43, A DECLARATION OF INTENT, no. 44, THE VOWS, nos. 45-46, AN EXCHANGE OF RINGS, nos. 47-48, PRAYERS, nos. 49-50, and concludes with THE LORD'S PRAYER and a BLESSING, no. 51.

RITE FOR
CELEBRATING MARRIAGE OUTSIDE MASS[13]

Entrance Rite and Liturgy of the Word

39 At the appointed time, the priest, wearing surplice and white stole [or a white cope, if desired], proceeds with the ministers to the door of the church or, if more suitable, to the altar. There he greets the bride and bridegroom in a friendly manner, showing that the Church shares their joy.

Where it is desirable that the rite of welcome be omitted, the celebration of matrimony begins at once with the liturgy of the word.

40 If there is a procession to the altar, the ministers go first, followed by the priest, and then the bride and bridegroom. According to local custom, they may be escorted by at least their parents and the two witnesses. Meanwhile, the entrance song is sung.

Then the people are greeted, and the prayer is offered, unless a brief pastoral exhortation seems more desirable.[14]

41 The liturgy of the word takes place in the usual manner. There may be three readings, the first of them from the Old Testament. [see nos. 67-105]

According to the words of the Constitution on the Sacred Liturgy, **Sacrosanctum Concilium**, repeated in no. 6 of the introduction above, the celebration of marriage normally takes place during Mass. Nevertheless, a good reason can excuse from the celebration of Mass (Sacred Congregation of Rites, Instruction, **Inter Oecumenici**, no. 70: AAS 56 [1964] 893), and sometimes even urges that Mass should be omitted. In this case the rite for celebrating marriage outside Mass should be used.

[14] II Vatican Council, Sacred Congregation of Rites, Instruction, **Inter Oecumenici**, no. 70: AAS 56 (1964) 894.

42 After the gospel, the priest gives a homily drawn from the sacred text. He speaks about the mystery of Christian marriage, the dignity of wedded love, the grace of the sacrament, and the responsibilities of married people, keeping in mind the circumstances of this particular marriage.

Rite of Marriage

43 All stand, including the bride and bridegroom, and the priest addresses them in these or similar words:

My dear friends, you have come together in this church so that the Lord may seal and strengthen your love in the presence of the Church's minister and this community. Christ abundantly blesses this love. He has already consecrated you in baptism and now he enriches and strengthens you by a special sacrament so that you may assume the duties of marriage in mutual and lasting fidelity. And so, in the presence of the Church, I ask you to state your intentions.

44 The priest them questions them about their freedom of choice, faithfulness to each other, and the acceptance and upbringing of children:

.... and ...., have you come here freely and without reservation to give yourselves to each other in marriage?

Will you love and honor each other as man and wife for the rest of your lives?

The following question may be omitted if, for example, the couple is advanced in years.

Will you accept children lovingly from God, and bring them up according to the law of Christ and his Church?

Each answers the questions separately.

Consent

45 The priest invites them to declare their consent:

Since it is your intention to enter into marriage, join your right hands, and declare your consent before God and his Church.

They join hands.
The bridegroom says:

I, ..., take you, ..., to be my wife. I promise to be true to you in good times and in bad, in sickness and in health. I will love you and honor you all the days of my life.

The bride says:

I, ..., take you, ..., to be my husband. I promise to be true to you in good times and in bad, in sickness and in health. I will love you and honor you all the days of my life.

If, however, it seems preferable for pastoral reasons, the priest may obtain consent from the couple through questions. First he asks the bridegroom:

.........., do you take .... to be your wife? Do you promise to be true to her in good times and in bad, in sickness and in health, to love her and honor her all the days of your life?

The bridegroom:

I do.

Then he asks the bride:

.........., do you take .... to be your husband? Do you promise to be true to him in good times and in bad, in sickness and in health, to love him and honor him all the days of your life?

The bride:

I do.

If pastoral necessity demands it, the conference of bishops may decree, in virtue of the faculty in no. 17, that the priest should always obtain the consent of the couple through questions.

In the dioceses of the Unites States, the following form may also be used:

I, ..., take you, ..., for my lawful wife, to have and to hold, from this day forward, for better, for worse, for richer, for poorer in sickness and in health, until death do us part.

I, ..., take you, ..., for my lawful husband, to have and to hold, from this day forward, for better, for worse, for richer, for poorer, in sickness and in health, until death do us part.

If it seems preferable for pastoral reasons for the priest to obtain consent from the couple through questions, in the dioceses of the United States the following alternative form may be used:

.........., do you take .... for your lawful wife (husband), to have and to hold, from this day forward, for better, for worse, for richer, for poorer, in sickness and in health, until death do you part?

The bride [bridegroom]; I do.

46 Receiving their consent, the priest says:

You have declared your consent before the Church. May the Lord in his goodness strengthen your consent and fill you both with his blessings.

What God has joined, men must not divide.

R Amen.

Blessing and Exchange of Rings

47 Priest:

May the Lord bless (+) these rings which you give to each other as the sign of your love and fidelity.

R Amen.

For other forms of the blessing of rings, see nos. 110, 111.

48 The bridegroom places his wife's ring on her ring finger.

.........., take this ring as a sign of my love and fidelity. In the name of the Father, and of the Son, and of the Holy Spirit.

The bride places her husband's ring on his ring finger. She may say:

.........., take this ring as a sign of my love and fidelity. In the name of the Father, and of the Son, and of the Holy Spirit.

General Intercessions and Nuptial Blessings

49 The general intercessions [prayer of the faithful] and the blessing of the couple take place in this order:

a] First the priest uses the invitatory of any blessing of the couple [see the first part of no. 33, 120, 121] or any other, taken from the approved formulas for the general intercessions.

b] Immediately after the invitatory, there can be either a brief silence, or a series of petitions from the prayer of the faithful with responses by the people. All the petitions should be in harmony with the blessing which follows, but should not duplicate it.

c] Then, omitting the prayer that concludes the prayer of the faithful, the priest extends his hands and blesses the bride and bridegroom.

50 This blessing may be Father, by your power, [no. 33 or another from nos. 120, 121.

Conclusion of the Celebration

51 The entire rite can be concluded with the Lord's Prayer and the blessing, whether with the simple form, May almighty God, or with one of the forms in nos. 125-127.

52 If two or more marriages are celebrated at the same time, the questioning before the consent, the consent itself, and the acceptance of consent shall always be done individually for each couple; the rest, including the nuptial blessing, is said once for all, using the plural form.

53 The rite described above should be used by a deacon who, when a priest cannot be present, has been delegated by the bishop or pastor to assist at the celebration of marriage, and to give the Chruch's blessing. [15]

[15] Paul VI, motu proprio, Sacram Diaconatus Ordinem, June 18, 1967, no. 22, 4: AAS 59 (1967) 702.

54 If Mass cannot be celebrated and communion is to be distributed during the rite, the Lord's Prayer is said first. After communion, a reverent silence may be observed for a while, or a psalm or song of praise may be sung or recited. Then comes the prayer, Lord, we who have shared (**no. 123, if only the bride and bridegroom receive) or the prayer,** God, who in this wondrous sacrament **or other suitable prayer.**

The rite ends with a blessing, either the simple formula, May almighty God bless you, **or one of the forms in nos. 125-127.**

TEXTS FOR USE IN THE MARRIAGE RITE AND IN THE WEDDING MASS

I. Scripture Readings

In the wedding Mass and in marriages celebrated without Mass, the following selections may be used:

Old Testament Readings

67	Genesis 1:26-28, 31a	Male and female he created them.
68	Genesis 2:18-24	And they will be two in one flesh.
69	Genesis 24:48-51 58-67	Isaac loved Rebekah, and so he was consoled for the loss of his mother.
70	Tobit 7:9c-10 11c-17 (Vulgate)	May God join you together and fill you with his blessings.
71	Tobit 8:5-10	May God bring us to old age together.
72	Song of Songs 2:8-10, 14, 16a; 8:6-7a	For love is as strong as death.

73 Ecclesiasticus 26:1-4, 16-21 (Greed 1-4, 13-16)

Like the sun rising is the beauty of a good wife in a well-kept house.

74 Jeremiah 31:31-32a, 33-34a

I will make a new convenant with the House of Israel and Judah.

New Testament Readings

75 Romans 8:31b-35, 37-39

Who will separate us from the love of Christ?

76 Romans 12:1-2, 9-18 (longer)

Offer to God your bodies as a living and holy sacrifice, truly pleasing to him.

77 1 Corinthians 6-13c-15a, 17-20

Your body is a temple of the Spirit.

78 1 Corinthians 12:31-13:8a

If I am without love, it will do me no good whatever.

79 Ephasians 5:2a, 21-33 (longer) or 2a, 25-32 (shorter)

This mystery has many implications, and I am saying it applies to Christ and the Church.

80 Colossians 3:12-17

Above all have love, which is the bond of perfection.

81 1 Peter 3:1-9

You should agree with one another, be sympathetic and love the brothers.

82 1 John 3:18-24

Our love is to be something real and active.

83 1 John 4:7-12

God is love.

84 Revelation 19:1, 5-9a

Happy are those who are invited to the wedding feast of the Lamb.

Responsorial Psalms

85 Psalm 32:12 and 18, 20-21, 22
  R [5b] The earth is full of the goodness of the
  Lord.
86 Psalm 33:2-3, 4-5, 6-7, 8-9
  R [2a] I will bless the Lord at all times.
  OR: [9a] Taste and see the goodness of the Lord.
87 Psalm 102:1-2, 8 and 13, 17-18a
  R [8a] The Lord is kind and merciful.
  OR: [17] The Lord's kindness is everlasting to
  those who fear him.
88 Psalm 111:1-2, 3-4, 5-7a, 7bc-8, 9
  R Happy are those who do what the Lord
  commands.
  OR: Alleluia.
89 Psalm 127:1-2, 3, 4-5
  R [1a] Happy are those who fear the Lord.
  OR: [4] See how the Lord blesses those who fear
  him.
90 Psalm 144:8-9, 10 and 15, 17-18
  R [9a] The Lord is compassionate to all his
  creatures.
91 Psalm 148:1-2, 3-4, 9-10, 11-12ab, 12c-14a
  R [12c] Let all praise the name of the Lord.
  OR: Alleluia.

Alleluia Verse and Verse before the Gospel

92 1 John 4:8 and 11   God is love; let us love one
                        another as he has loved us.
93 1 John 4:12   If we love one another God
                        will live in us in perfect
                        love.
94 1 John 4:16   He who lives in love, lives
                        in God, and God in him.
95 1 John 4:7b   Everyone who loves is
                        born of God and knows
                        him.

Gospels

96 Matthew 5:1-12 — Rejoice and be glad, for your reward will be great in heaven.

97 Matthew 5:13-16 — You are the light of the world.

98 Matthew 7:21, 24-29 (longer) 21, 24-25 (shorter) — He built his house on rock.

99 Matthew 19:3-6 — So then, what God has united, man must not divide.

100 Matthew 22:35-40 — This is the greatest and the first commandment. The second is similar to it.

101 Mark 10:6-9 — They are no longer two, therefore, but one body.

102 John 2:1-11 — This was the first of the signs given by Jesus; it was given at Cana in Galilee.

103 John 15:9-12 — Remain in my love.

104 John 15:12-16 — This is my commandment: love one another.

105 John 17:20-26 (longer) 20-23 (shorter) — May they be completely one.

II. OPENING PRAYERS

1

106 Father,
you have made the bond of marriage
a holy mystery,
a symbol of Christ's love for his Church.
Hear our prayers for .... and ....
With faith in you and in each other
they pledge their love today.
May their lives always bear witness
to the reality of that love.

We ask you this through our Lord Jesus Christ,
your Son,
With faith in you and in each other
they pledge their love today.
May their lives always bear witness
to the reality of that love.

We ask you this through our Lord Jesus Christ,
your Son,
Who lives and reigns with you and the Holy Spirit,
one God, for ever and ever.

2

107 Father,
hear our prayers for .... and ....
who today are united in marriage before your altar.
Give them your blessing,
and strengthen their love for each other.

We ask you this through our Lord . . .

3

108 Almighty God,
hear our prayers for .... and ....,
who have come here today

to be untied in the sacrament of marriage.
Increase their faith in you and in each other,
and through them bless your Church
(with Christian children).

We ask you this
through our Lord ...

4

109 Father,
when you created mankind
you willed that man and wife should be one.
Bind .... and ....
in the loving union of marriage;
and make their love fruitful
so that they may be living witnesses
to your divine love in the world.

We ask you this
through our Lord ...

III. BLESSING OF RINGS

1

110 Lord, bless these rings which we bless + in
your name.
Grant that those who wear them
may always have a deep faith in each other.
May they do your will
and always live together
in peace, good will, and love.

(We ask this) through Christ our Lord.
R Amen.

2

111 Lord,
bless + and consecrate .... and ....
in their love for each other.
May these rings be a symbol
of true faith in each other,
and always remind them of their love.

(We ask this) through Christ our Lord.
R Amen.

Nuptial Blessing

1

33 The priest faces the bride and bridegroom and, with hands joined, says:
My dear friends, let us turn to the Lord and pray that he will bless with his grace this woman (or ....) now married in Christ to this man (or ....) and that (through the sacrament of the body and blood of Christ,) he will unite in love the couple he has joined in this holy bond. **All pray silently for a short while. Then the priest extends his hands and continues:**
Father, by your power you have made everything out of nothing. In the beginning you created the universe and made mankind in your own likeness. You gave man the constant help of woman so that man and woman should no longer be two, but one flesh, and you teach us that what you have united may never be divided.
Father, you have made the union of man and wife so holy a mystery that it symbolizes the marriage of Christ and his Church.
Father, by your plan man and woman are united, and married life has been established as the one blessing that was not forfeited by original sin or washed away in the flood.
Look with love upon this woman, your daughter, now joined to her husband in marriage. She asks your

blessing. Give her the grace of love and peace. May she always follow the example of the holy women whose praises are sung in the scriptures.

May her husband put his trust in her and recognize that she is his equal and the heir with him to the life of grace. May he always honor her and love her as Christ loves his bride, the Church.

Father, keep them always true to your commandments. Keep them faithful in marriage and let them be living examples of Christian life. Give them the strength which comes from the gospel so that they may be witnesses of Christ to others. (Bless them with children and help them to be good parents. May they live to see their children's children.) And, after a happy old age, grant them fullness of life with the saints in the kingdom of heaven.

(We ask this) through Christ our Lord.

R Amen.

34 If one or both of the parties will not be receiving communion, the words in the introduction to the nuptial blessing, through the sacrament of the body and blood of Christ, **may be omitted.**

If desired, in the prayer Father, by your power, **two of the first three paragraphs may be omitted, keeping only the paragraph which corresponds to the reading of the Mass.**

In the last paragraph of this prayer, the words in parentheses may be omitted whenever circumstances suggest it, if, for example, the couple is advanced in years.

Other forms of the nuptial blessing:

2

120 In the following prayer, either the paragraph Holy Father, you created mankind, **or the paragraph** Father, to reveal the plan of your love, **may be omitted, keeping only the paragraph which corresponds to the reading.**

The priest faces the bride and bridegroom and, with hands joined, says:

Let us pray to the Lord for .... and .... who come to God's altar at the beginning of their married life so that they may always be united in love for each other (as now they share in the body and blood of Christ).

All pray silently for a short while. Then the priest extends his hands and continues:

Holy Father, you created mankind in your own image and made man and woman to be joined as husband and wife in union of body and heart and so fulfill their mission in this world.

Father, to reveal the plan of your love, you made the union of husband and wife an image of the covenant between you and your people. In the fulfillment of this sacrament, the marriage of Christian man and woman is a sign of the marriage between Christ and the Church. Father, stretch out your hand, and bless .... and ....

Lord, grant that as they begin to live this sacrament they may share with each other the gifts of your love and become one in heart and mind as witnesses to your presence in their marriage. Help them to create a home together (and give them children to be formed by the gospel and to have a place in your family).

Give your blessings to .... , your daughter, so that she may be a good wife (and mother), caring for the home, faithful in love for her husband, generous and kind. Give your blessings to ...., your son, so that he may be a faithful husband (and a good father).

Father, grant that as they come together to your table on earth, so they may one day have the joy of sharing your feast in heaven.

(We ask this) through Christ our Lord.

R Amen.

3

The priest faces the bride and bridegroom and, with

hands joined, says:

121 My dear friends, let us ask God for his continued blessings upon this bridegroom and his bride (or .... and ....).

All pray silently for a short while. Then the priest extends his hands and continues:

Holy Father, creator of the universe, maker of man and woman in you own likeness, source of blessing for married life, we humbly pray to you for this woman who today is united with her husband in this sacrament of marriage. May your fullest blessing come upon her and her husband so that they may together rejoice in your gift of married love (and enrich your Chruch with their children).

Lord, may they both praise you when they are happy and turn to you in their sorrows. May they be glad that you help them in their work and know that you are with them in their need. May they pray to you in the community of the Church, and be your witnesses in the world. May they reach old age in the company of their friends, and come at last to the kingdom of heaven.

(We ask this) through Christ our Lord.

R Amen.

BLESSING AT THE END OF MASS

1

. **125** God the eternal Father keep you in love with each other, so that the peace of Christ may stay with you and be always in your home.

R Amen.

May (your children bless you,) your friends console you and all men live in peace with you.

R Amen.

May you always bear witness to the love of God in this world so that the afflicted and the needy will find in you generous friends, and welcome you into the joys of heaven.

R Amen.

And may almighty God bless you all, the Father, and the Son, + and the Holy Spirit.

R Amen.

2

126 May God, the almighty Father, give you his joy and bless you (in your children).

R Amen.

May the only Son of God have mercy on you and help you in good times and in bad.

R Amen.

May the Holy Spirit Of God always fill your hearts with his love.

R Amen.

And may almighty God bless you all, the Father, and the Son, + and the Holy Spirit.

R Amen.

3

127 May the Lord Jesus, who was a guest at the wedding in Cana, bless you and your families and friends.

R Amen.

May Jesus, who loved his Church to the end, always fill your hearts with his love.

R Amen.

May he grant that, as you believe in his resurrection, so you may wiat for him in joy and hope.

R Amen.

And may almighty God bless you all, the Father, and the Son, + and the Holy Spirit.

R Amen.

MARRIAGE SERVICE MATERIALS
ARRANGED FOR COMPARISON

In this chapter you will find the various parts of the preceding ten services arranged for comparison. In some places more materials have been added in order to give you a wider selection. The materials presented in this book are only a selection. The variety which can be used is almost limitless, so please do not feel that you are limited to the materials presented here. In some cases the same prayers, etc., are used in more than one service. In this case two numbers will appear beside the item.

Calls to Worship

E1 Let us worship God. There was a marriage at Cana in Galilee. Jesus was invited to the marriage with his disciples.

H1 Our Lord Jesus said: from the beginning of creation, God made them male and female. For this reason a man shall leave his father and mother and be joined to his wife, so they are no longer two but one.

I1 We are gathered here to worship God and to witness the marriage vows of .... and .... Let your light so shine before men that they may see your good works and give glory to your Father who is in heaven.

206 Then the Lord God said, It is not good that the man should be alone. I will make a helper fit for him.

207 Jesus said, Abide in me, and I in you. As the branch cannot bear fruit by itself, unless it abides in the vine, neither can you unless you abide in me.

208 Beloved, let us love one another, for love is of God, and he who loves is born of God and knows God. He who does not love does not know God, for God is love.

Invocations

B3 The Lord be with you.
And also with you.

Let us pray.

Eternal God, creator and sustainer of all men, giver of all grace, author of salvation: Look with favor upon this man and this woman, that they may grow in love and peace together, through Jesus Christ your Son our Lord, who lives and reigns with you in the unity of the Holy Spirit, one God, now and forever. Amen.

D2 Let us pray.

Almighty and ever-blessed God, whose presence is the happiness of every condition, and whose favor hallows every relation, we beseech thee to be present and favorable unto these thy servants, that they may be truly joined in the honorable estate of marriage, and in covenant with thee, O God. As thou hast brought them together by thy providence, sanctify them by thy Spirit, giving them a new frame of heart fit for their new estate, and enrich them with all grace, whereby they may enjoy the comforts, undergo the cares, endure the trials, and perform the duties of life together as Christians, under thy heavenly guidance and protection, through our Lord Jesus Christ. Amen.

G1 In the name of the Father, the Son, and the Holy Spirit. Amen.

Let us pray

Eternal God, in your love and divine wisdom you have created us male and female so that we may be joined in marriage and know the love and joy you have prepared for us. We pray that you will be present and look with favor upon .... and .... your servants who now come before you to be joined as husband and wife. Send your Spirit upon them that they may know the joy of your guiding presence through all the days of their life together. Amen.

H2 Let us pray.

Almighty God, whose presence is the happiness of every condition, and whose favor makes all our relationships holy, we ask you to be present and look with favor upon .... and .... , that they may be joined in

Christian marriage, as they make their promises in your presence.

Eternal God, since you are our creator and give us the very breath of life, we ask you to guide these two in their life together. Give them a spirit of love and faithfulness, which will allow them to share the love, undergo the cares, endure the trials, and perform the duties of life together as Christians, under your divine guidance and protection, through Jesus Christ our Lord. Amen.

106 Father, you have made the bond of marriage a holy mystery, a symbol of Christ's love for his Church. Hear our prayers for .... and .... With faith in you and in each other they pledge their love today. May their lives always bear witness to the reality of that love. We ask you this through our Lord Jesus Christ, your Son, who lives and reigns with you and the Holy Spirit, one God, for ever and ever.

107 Father, hear our prayers for .... and ...., who today are united in marriage before your altar. Give them your blessing, and strengthen their love for each other. We ask you this through our Lord . . .

108 Almighty God, hear our prayers for .... and ...., who have come here today to be united in the sacrament of marriage. Increase their faith in you and in each other, and through them bless your Church (with Christian children). We ask you this through our Lord . . .

109 Father, when you created mankind you willed that man and wife should be one. Bind .... and .... in the loving union of marriage; and make their love fruitful so that they may be living witnesses to your divine love in the world. We ask you this through our Lord . . .

209 Almighty God, unto whom all hearts are open, all desires known, and from whom no secrets are hid, cleanse the thoughts of our hearts by the inspiration of thy Holy Spirit, that we may perfectly love thee, and worthily magnify thy holy name, through Jesus Christ our Lord.

210 O God, from whom all holy desires, all good counsels, and all just works do proceed, Give unto thy servants .... and .... that peace which the world cannot give, that their hearts may be set to obey thy commandments, and also that by thee, we, being defended from fear and unbelief, may pass our time in rest and quietness, through Jesus Christ our Lord.

211 Father, when you created mankind you willed that man and wife should be one. Bind .... and .... in the loving union of marriage, and make their love fruitful so that they may be living witnesses to your divine love in the world. We ask this through Jesus Christ our Lord.

212 Eternal God in whom we live and move and have our being, we pray that you will look with favor upon .... and .... who now stand before you. Send your Spirit upon them and consecrate this moment that they may be joined as husband and wife under the direction of your divine purposes, through Jesus Christ our Lord.

213 Almighty God, maker and preserver of all things visible and invisible, we adore your infinite majesty, and we bless your name for the revelation of your love in Jesus Christ our Lord. Look with favor now upon .... and .... who filled with human love, now turn to you for the blessing of divine love upon their marriage, through Jesus Christ our Lord.

Prayers of Confession

E3 Almighty God, our Father, you created us for life together. We confess that we have turned from your will. We have not loved one another as you commanded. We have been quick to claim our own rights and careless of the rights of others. We have taken much and given little. Forgive our disobedience, O God, and strengthen us in love, so that we may serve you as a faithful people, and live together in your joy, through Jesus Christ our Lord.

I2 Eternal God we do not presume to offer anything

to you that is worthy of your love and righteousness. We offer ourselves, in all our imperfection, in our sins and selfishness. Forgive us, Father, and help us to forgive one another as you forgive us.

At this joyous time help us to commit ourselves to the meaning and the mystery of marriage. Help us to stand with .... and .... as they begin a new relationship under your divine guidance. Lead us all to practice the love and forgiveness which will strengthen this marriage, through Jesus Christ our Lord.

214 Almighty God, thou who hast sent thine only Son Jesus Christ to deliver us from our sin and empty living, make real in our hearts the promises of love, brotherly affection and new life, that thou hast revealed to us. Cleanse our lives from everything that would hinder our perfect and true response to thy loving call, for we pray in the name of Jesus Christ our Savior and Lord.

215 Lord, we have sinned against you. Lord, have mercy.

Lord, have mercy.

Lord, show us your mercy and love.

And grant us your salvation.

216 Eternal God, our Father, you are from everlasting, you have made us and not we ourselves. You have set us but a short distance from you that we may learn your ways, and love you with all our hearts. Forgive us, when in fear and selfishness we turn from doing your will and seek something else. Help us to renew and make strong those promises we have made to you, that we will be renewed and remade on the inside as well as on the outside, through our Lord Jesus Christ.

217 Most merciful God, we confess that we have sinned against you in thought, word, and deed. We have not loved you with our whole heart. We have not loved our neighbors as ourselves. We pray you of your mercy, forgive what we have been, amend what we are, direct what we shall be, that we may delight in your will, and walk in your ways, through Jesus Christ our Lord.

Declarations of Pardon

E4 Here and believe the good news of the Gospel. Nothing can separate us from the love of God in Christ Jesus our Lord.

In Jesus we are forgiven.

I3 Jesus Christ has died for our sins, and in him, God grants us forgiveness. Believe this good news, accept his forgiveness, and turn to serve him. Make his way, your way. Amen.

218 Almighty God, who doth freely pardon all who repent and turn to him, now fulfill in every contrite heart the promise of redeeming grace, remitting all our sins, and cleansing us from an evil conscience, through the perfect sacrifice of Christ Jesus our Lord.

219 Hear now the assurance of the words of Holy Scripture, "For God so loved the world that he gave his only Son, that whoever believes in him should not perish, but have eternal life. For God sent the Son into the world, not to condemn the world, but that the world might be saved through him."

220 God shows his love for us in that while we were yet sinners Christ died for us. Therefore, if anyone is in Christ he is a new creation, the old has passed away, behold the new has come. The mercy of the Lord is from everlasting to everlasting, therefore we can believe in the name of Jesus Christ, that we are forgiven.

221 May almighty God have mercy on us, forgive us our sins, and bring us to everlasting life.

222 Almighty God have mercy on you, forgive you all your sins, through our Lord Jesus Christ, strengthen you in all goodness, and by the power of the Holy Spirit keep you in eternal life.

Scripture Readings

Psalms
100
113
127
128

Old Testament Readings
Genesis 2:4-9, 15-24
Genesis 24:48-67
Song of Solomon 2:8-15
Isaiah 55:1-9

148

| Gospel Readings | Jeremiah 31:31-34 |
| | Epistle Readings |

Gospel Readings
  Matthew 5:1-12
  Matthew 22:34-40
  Matthew 5:24-27
  Mark 10:6-9
  John 15:11-17

Jeremiah 31:31-34
Epistle Readings
  Romans 8:31-39
  1 Corinthians 13:1-13
  Ephesians 5:21-33
  Colossians 3:12-17
  1 John 4:7-12

Introductory Statements

A1 Dearly beloved, we are gathered together here in the sight of God, and in the face of this company, to join together this man and this woman in holy matrimony, which is an honorable estate, instituted of God, signifying unto us the mystical union that is betwixt Christ and his Church, which holy estate Christ adorned and beautified with his presence and first miracle which he wrought in Cana of Galilee, and is commended of Saint Paul to be honorable among all men, and therefore is not by any to be entered into unadvisedly or lightly but reverently, discreetly, advisedly, soberly, and in the fear of God. Into this holy estate these two persons present come now to be joined. If any man can show just cause why they may not lawfully be joined together, let him now speak, or else hereafter forever hold his peace.

I require and charge you both, as ye will answer at the dreadful day of judgment when the secrets of all hearts shall be disclosed, that if either of you know any impediment, why ye may not be lawfully joined together in matrimony, ye do now confess it. For be ye well assured that if any persons are joined together otherwise than as God's Word doth allow, their marriage is not lawful.

8 Good people, we have come together in the presence of God to witness and proclaim the joining together of this man and this woman in marriage. The bond of marriage was established by God at creation, and our Lord Jesus Christ himself adorned this manner of life by his presence and first miracle at a wedding in Cana of Galilee. It signifies to us the union between Christ and his Church, and Holy Scripture commands it to be honored among all men.

The union of man and woman in heart, body, and mind is intended by God for their mutual joy; for the help and comfort given one another in prosperity and adversity; and, when it is God's will; for the procreation of children and their nuture in the knowledge and love of the Lord. Therefore marriage is not to be entered into unadvisedly or lightly, but reverently, deliberately, and in accord with the purposes for which it was instituted by God. Into this holy union .... and .... come now to be joined. If any of you can show just cause why they may not lawfully be married, speak now, or forever hold your peace.

I require and charge you both in the name of God, that if either of you know any reason why you may not be united in marriage lawfully and in accordance with God's Word, you confess it now.

C1 Dearly beloved, we are gathered together here in the sight of God, and in the presence of these witnesses to join together .... and .... in holy matrimony; which is an honorable estate, instituted of God, and signifying unto us the mystical union which exists between Christ and his Church; which holy estate Christ adorned and beautified with his presence in Cana of Galilee. It is therefore not to be entered into unadvisedly, but reverently, discreetly, and in the fear of God. Into this holy estate these two persons come now to be joined. If any man can show just cause why they may not lawfully be joined together, let him now speak, or else hereafter forever hold his peace.

I require and charge you both, as you stand in the presence of God, before whom the secrets of all hearts are disclosed, that, having duly considered the holy covenant you are about to make, you do now declare before this company your pledge of faith, each to the other. Be well assured that if these solemn vows are kept inviolate, as God's Word demands, and if steadfastly you endeavor to do the will of your heavenly Father, God will bless your marriage, will grant you fulfillment in it, and will establish your home in peace.

D1 Dearly beloved, we are assembled here in the presence of God, to join this man and this woman in holy marriage, which is instituted by God, regulated by his commandments, blessed by our Lord Jesus Christ, and to be held in honor among all men. Let us reverently remember that God has established and sanctified marriage, for the welfare and happiness of mankind. Our savior has declared that a man shall leave his father and mother and cleave unto his wife. By his apostles, he has instructed those who enter this relationship to cherish a mutual esteem and love; to bear with each other's infirmities and weaknesses; to comfort each other in sickness, trouble, and sorrow; to provide for each other, and for their household in temporal things; to pray for and encourage each other in the things which pertain to God; to live together as heirs of the grace of life.

I charge you both before God, the searcher of hearts, that if you know any reason why you may not be joined in marriage, you say so; for God is a God of truth.

E2 Friends, marriage is established by God. In marriage a man and a woman willingly bind themselves together in love and become one even as Christ is one with the church, his body.

Let marriage be held in honor among all.

F1 In the name of the Father, and of the Son, and of the Holy Ghost. Amen.

Dearly beloved, forasmuch as marriage is a holy estate, ordained of God, and to be held in honor by all, it becometh those who enter therein to weigh, with reverent minds, what the Word of God teacheth concerning it.

The Lord God said: It is not good that the man should be alone; I will make him a help meet for him.

Our Lord Jesus Christ said: Have ye not read that he which them at the beginning made them male and female, and said, For this cause shall a man leave his father and mother, and shall cleave to his wife, and they twain shall be one flesh? Wherefore, they are no more twain, but one flesh. What therefore God hath joined together, let no man put asunder.

G2 Friends, God in his love and goodness toward us has given us marriage to be a precious gift. Through this gift we can know the deepest human relationship, one which almost touches heaven itself. It is through this precious gift that God raises up for himself new life, to be children of the covenant, praising his name and making visible his holy will.

God has created us male and female to walk together, side by side. In marriage two individuals become one flesh, united in love, in purpose, and in spirit. As our Lord taught us, "From the beginning of creation God made them male and female. For this reason a man shall leave his father and mother and be joined to his wife, and the two shall become one. So they are no longer two but one. What therefore God has joined together, let not man put asunder."

Marriage is sacred and holy, and it requires more of two individuals than they in their own strength can offer. God in his infinite mercy knows our weakness and has given us his Spirit to guide us and empower us so that we can be what he calls us to be.

.... and .... if you will rely upon the power and promises God gives us, you will know a deeper love, a more vital relationship, and a harmony of life which will lead you through all the trials and adversities you may face.

H3 Friends, we are gathered here in the presence of God to join .... and .... in holy marriage. For Chirstians, marriage is instituted of God, and it is holy. Marriage is to be regualted by his commandments, for through them we live as we were created to live. Marriage is blessed by our Lord Jesus Christ, and we believe that it is to be held in honor by all men.

God, our heavenly father has established marriage for our welfare and our happiness. Through Jesus Christ we are told that a man shall leave his father and mother and live as one with his wife. Through the teachings of the apostles, Jesus has instructed those who marry to love each other, to be patient and kind with each other's problems and weaknesses, to comfort each other in sorrow and sickness, to provide for each other and for their children the things which pertain to earthly life, and to pray for and encourage each other in the worship and service of God, and in those things which are eternal.

.... and .... if you will do these things you will know love and joy and eternal happiness.

14 .... and .... you are entering into a new experience and a holy relationship. "It is a chief moment in life when two people, who were strangers to one another, are drawn together by and irresistible attraction, so that their souls cannot be henceforth divided by time or space; when one sees in a single woman that dream of purity and sweetness which has ever haunted his soul; when in a single man she finds the rest and satisfaction her heart has been unconsciously seeking. It is a revelation from above, and makes all things new; it is the hand of Providence, and annuls every argument of worldly providence.

You are performing an act of utter faith, believing in one another to the end.

As the bride gives herself to the bridegroom, let him be to her now father and mother, sister and brother, and most sacred — husband. As he gives himself to her, let the bride sustain and inspire his heart in the great affairs of life and in his chosen calling.

If you wish your new estate to be touched with perennial beauty, cherish those gracious visions which have made spring within your hearts during the days of your betrothal. You must never forget nor deny the vision you once saw; you must resolve that it be not blotted or blurred by the commonplace experiences of life. Faults may appear which were once hidden in a golden mist; excellencies may seem to fade in the glare of the noonday sun. Still be unmoved in your devotion; still remain confident and hopeful. Amid the reality of present imperfection, believe in the ideal. You saw it once. It still exists. It is the final truth.

This is the man, that is the woman you love. That is the shape of spiritual beauty God sees and which for an hour he showed to you. That is the soul which is to be when this conflict with temptations, hindrances, failures is accomplished. Hide that imagination in your inmost heart. Make real this ideal in your united lives and your home will be a 'place of repair and habor,' a dwelling place of contentment and abiding joy, a foretaste of that heavenly habitation where goodness reigns and love is the very air, the kingdom and home of our Father above. Amen."

43 My dear friends, you have come together in this church so that the Lord may seal and strengthen your love in the presence of the Church's minister and this community. Christ abundantly blesses this love. He has already consecrated you in baptism and now he enriches and strengthens you by a speical sacrament so that you may assume the duties of marriage in a mutual and lasting fidelity. And so, in the presence of the Church, I ask you to state your intentions.

223 We are gathered here to witness the marriage of .... and .... A marriage is not just a few words or some names on a piece of paper. Our Lord Jesus Christ has told us that a man shall leave his father and mother and be joined to his wife. We are here to confirm that truth. Holy vows taken in the presence of God are the fruit of a growing love, and they are also the beginning of a new relationship, a deepening of love, and the establishing of a new home. Let us rejoice with .... and .... at this most happy and holy time.

Declarations of Intent

A2, C2, and F3 .... wilt thou have this woman to thy wedded wife, to live together after God's ordinance in the holy estate of matrimony? Wilt thou love her, comfort her, honor, and keep her in sickness and in health; and, forsaking all others, keep thee only unto her, so long as ye both shall live?

B .... wilt thou have this man to thy wedded husband, to live together after God's ordinance in the holy estate of matrimony? Wilt thou love him, comfort him, honor, and keep him in sickness and in health; and, forsaking all others, keep thee only unto him, so long as ye both shall live?

B2 G .... will you have this woman to be your wife, to live together in a holy marriage? Will you love her, comfort her, honor and keep her, in sickness and in health, and forsaking all others, be faithful to her as long as you both shall live?

I will by God's help.

B .... will you have this man to be your husband to live together in a holy marriage? Will you love him, comfort him, honor and keep him in sickness and in health, and forsaking all others, be faithful to him as long as you both shall live?

I will by God's help.

D3 G .... wilt thou have this woman to be thy wife, and wilt thou pledge thy troth to her, in all love and honor, in all duty and service, in all faith and tenderness, to live with her, and cherish her, according to the ordinance of God, in the holy bond of marriage?

B .... wilt thou have this man to be thy wedded husband, and wilt thou pledge thy troth to him in all love and honor, in all duty and service, in all faith and tenderness, to live with him, and cherish him, according to the ordinance of God, in the holy bond of marriage?

G3 The minister will address first the man, then the woman, and finally the parents of both.

.... do you desire to be united in marriage with ...., and will you love her, comfort her, honor her, and be her helper as long as you both shall live?

I do and I will.

.... do you desire to be united in marriage with .... and will you love him, comfort him, honor him, and be his helper as long as you both shall live?

I do and I will.

The parents of the bride and groom will stand.
Will you the parents of .... and .... do all in your power to uphold their marriage in the years ahead, and will you promise to pray for and encourage them that they may fulfill the vows they are making today?
We will.

H4 G .... will you take **B** .... to be your wife, and will you be faithful to her, to love her, to honor her, to live with her and cherish her according to the commandments of God in holy marriage?

G .... will you take **B** .... to be your husband, and will you be faithful to him, to love him, to honor him, to live with him and cherish him according to the commandments of God in holy marriage?

I5 Christian marriage is most serious, because it will bind you together for life in a relationship so close and so intimate that the two of you will become one. Before you lies a future with its hopes and disappointments, its successes and its failures, its pleasures and its pains, its joys and its sorrows. These elements are mingled in every life and are to be expected; but for Christians they are not there to be received with resignation, but with hope and joy and all the spiritual gifts God's Spirit promises us.

G .... do you come here freely to take .... as your wife, according to the commandments of God in holy marriage?
I do

B .... do you come here freely to take .... as your husband, according to the commandments of God in holy marriage?
I do

44 the priest then questions them about their freedom of choice, faithfulness to each other, and the acceptance and upbringing of children:
.... and ...., have you come here freely and without reservation to give yourselves to each other in marriage? Will you love and honor each other as man and wife for the rest of your lives?

The **following** question **may be omitted if, for
example, the couple is advanced in years.**
Will you accept children lovingly from God, and bring
them up according to the law of Christ and his Church?
Each answers the questions separately.

Vows

A3, C3, and F4 I .... take thee .... to my wedded
wife, to have and to hold from this day forward, for
better for worse, for richer for poorer, in sickness and in
health, to love and to cherish, till death us do part,
according to God's holy ordinance, and thereto I
plight/pledge thee my troth/faith.

I .... take thee .... to my wedded husband, to
have and to hold from this day forward, for better for
worse, for richer for poorer, in sickness and in health, to
love and to cherish, till death us do part, according to
God's holy ordinance, and thereto I plight/pledge thee
my troth/faith.

12 I .... take you .... to be my wife, to have and
to hold from this day forward, for better for worse, for
richer for poorer, in sickness and in health, to love and to
cherish, until we are parted by death. This is my solemn
vow.

I .... take you .... to be my husband, to have
and to hold from this day forward, for better for worse,
for richer for poorer, in sickness and in health, to love
and to cherish, until we are parted by death. This is my
solemn vow.

D4 I .... take thee .... to be my wedded wife,
and I do promise and covenant, before God and these
witnesses, to be thy loving and faithful husband, in
plenty and in want, in joy and in sorrow, in sickness and
in health, as long as we both shall live.

I .... take thee .... to be my wedded husband,
and I do promise and covenant, before God and these
witnesses, to be thy loving and faithful wife, in plenty
and in want, in joy and in sorrow, in sickness and in
health, as long as we both shall live.

E5 .... I promise with God's help to be your faithful husband, to love and serve you as Christ commands, as long as we both shall live.

.... I promise with God's help to be your faithful wife, to love and serve you as Christ commands, as long as we both shall live.

F5 I .... take thee .... to my wedded wife, and plight thee my troth till death us do part.

I .... take thee .... to my wedded husband, and plight thee my troth, till death us do part.

G4 The wedding party will proceed to the altar where the bride and groom shall face each other and join hands.

.... and .... you are now about to commit yourselves to each other in the bonds of Christian marriage. This is the most solemn moment in a marriage service, for there you make your promises to God and to each other.

G .... I promise before God, our family, and friends to be your loving and faithful husband, to share my life with you, in wealth and in poverty, in sickness and in health, in good times and in bad times for as long as we both shall live.

B .... I promise before God, our family, and friends to be your loving and faithful wife, to share my life with you, in wealth and in poverty, in sickness and in health, in good times and in bad times for as long as we both shall live.

H5 .... I promise before God and these witnesses to be your loving and faithful husband, in joy and sorrow, through sickness and health, in times of plenty or want, as long as we both shall live.

.... I promise before God and these witnesses to be your loving and faithful wife, in joy and sorrow, through sickness and health, in times of plenty or want, as long as we both shall live.

I6 I .... take you .... to be my wife and I promise before God and these friends that I will share my life with you in all love and honor, in all faith and tenderness, through joy and sorrow, in sickness and health, as long as we both shall live.

I .... take you .... to by my husband and I promise before God and these friends that I will share my life with you in all love and honor, in all faith and tenderness, through joy and sorrow, in sickness and health, as long as we both shall live.

45 The priest invites them to declare their consent:

Since it is your intention to enter into marriage, join your right hands, and declare your consent before God and his Church.

They join hands. The bridegroom says:

I, ..., take you, ..., to be my wife. I promise to be true to you in good times and in bad, in sickness and in health. I will love you and honor you all the days of my life.

The bride says:

I, ..., take you, ..., to be my husband. I promise to be true to you in good times and in bad, in sickness and in health. I will love you and honor you all the days of my life.

If, however, it seems preferable for pastoral reasons, the priest may obtain consent from the couple through questions. First he asks the bridegroom:

.........., do you take .... to be your wife? Do you promise to be true to her in good times and in bad, in sickness and in health, to love her and honor her all the days of your life?

The bride:

I do.

If pastoral necessity demands it, the conference of bishops may decree, in virtue of the faculty in no. 17, that the priest should always obtain the consent of the couple through questions.

In the dioceses of the Unites States, the following form may also be used:

I, ..., take you, ..., for my lawful wife, to have and to hold, from this day forward, for better, for worse, for richer, for poorer in sickness and in health, until death do us part.

I, ..., take you, ..., for my lawful husband, to have and to hold, from this day forward, for better, for worse, for richer, for poorer, in sickness and in health, until death do us part.

If it seems preferable for pastoral reasons for the priest to obtain consent from the couple through questions, in the dioceses of the United States the following alternative form may be used:

.........., do you take .... for your lawful wife (husband), to have and to hold, from this day forward, for better, for worse, for richer, for poorer, in sickness and in health, until death do you part?

The bride [bridegroom]; I do.

46. Receiving their consent, the priest says:

You have declared your consent before the Church. May the Lord in his goodness strengthen your consent and fill you both with his blessings. What God has joined, men must not divide.

R. Amen.

Exchange of Rings

A4 and D5 Bless, O Lord, this ring, that he/she who gives it and she/he who wears it may abide in thy peace, and continue in thy favor, unto their life's end, through Jesus Christ our Lord. Amen.

With this ring I thee wed, in the name of the Father, and of the Son, and of the Holy Ghost. Amen.
or

This ring I give thee in token and pledge, of our constant faith and abiding love.

B6 Bless, O Lord, the ring that he/she who gives it and she/he who wears it may live in your peace, and continue in your favor, all the days of their life, through Jesus Christ our Lord. Amen.

.... I give you this ring as a symbol of my vow, and with all that I am, and all that I have, I honor you in the name of God.

C4 The wedding ring is the outward and visible sign of an inward and spiritual grace, signifying to all, the uniting of this man and woman in holy matrimony, through Jesus Christ our Lord.

Let us Pray.

Bless, O Lord, the giving of these rings, that they who wear them may abide in thy peace, and continue in thy favor, through Jesus Christ our Lord. Amen.

In token and pledge of our constant faith and abiding love, with this ring I thee wed, in the name of the Father, and of the Son, and of the Holy Spirit. Amen.

E6 I give you this ring as a sign of my promise.

F6 Receive this ring as a token of wedded love and troth.

G5 The man and the woman may exchange rings and say:

This ring is a symbol of my love and faithfulness.

H6 Eternal God, we pray for your blessing upon these rings that they may be a permanent reminder of holy promises and steadfast love. Bless these who wear them that they may remain in your favor throughout all their earthly life, through Jesus Christ our Lord. Amen.

This ring is the sign of my promise, and I give it to you in the name of the Father, and of the Son, and of the Holy Spirit. Amen.

I7 Eternal God, bless these rings that as .... and .... wear them they will be reminded of their faith in you and their promises to each other. Let these rings be symbols of a deep faith and an unending love, through Jesus Christ our Lord. Amen.

.... this ring is the sign of my love and faithfulness, and I give it to you in the name of the Father, the Son, and the Holy Spirit. Amen

47 Priest:

May the Lord bless + these rings which you give to each other as the sign of your love and fidelity.

R. Amen.

For other forms of the blessing of rings, see nos. 110, 111.

48 The bridegroom places his wife's ring on her ring finger. He may say:

.........., take this ring as a sign of my love and fidelity. In the name of the Father, and of the Son, and of the Holy Spirit.

The bride places her husband's ring on his ring finger. She may say:

.........., take this ring as a sign of my love and fidelity. In the name of the Father, and of the Son, and of the Holy Spirit.

224 What symbols do you give of these holy promises?

These rings

Do you **B** .... receive this ring as an outward pledge and symbol of your promise to fulfill these vows?

I do

Do you **G** .... receive this ring as an outward pledge and symbol of your promise to fulfill these vows?

I do

Declarations of Marriage

A8 Those whom God hath joined together let no man put asunder.

Forasmuch as .... and .... have consented together in holy wedlock, and have witnessed the same before God and this company, and thereto have given and pledged their troth, each to the other, and have declared the same by giving and receiving a ring, and by joining hands: I pronounce that they are man and wife, in the name of the Father, and the Son, and the Holy Ghost. Amen.

B7 Now that .... and .... have given themselves to each other by solemn vows, with the joining of hands and the giving and receiving of a ring (rings), I pronounce that they are husband and wife, in the name of the Father, and of the Son, and of the Holy Spirit.

Those whom God has joined together let not man put asunder.

C5 Forasmuch as .... and .... have consented together in holy wedlock, and have witnessed the same before God and this company and thereto have pledged their faith each to the other, and have declared the same by joining hands and by giving and receiving rings: I pronounce that they are husband and wife together, in the name of the Father, and of the Son, and of the Holy Spirit.

Those whom God hath joined together, let not man put asunder.

D7 By the authority committed unto me as a minister of the Church of Christ, I declare that .... and .... are now husband and wife according to the ordinance of God, and the law of the state, in the name of the Father, and of the Son, and of the Holy Spirit.

Whom therefore God has joined together, let no man put asunder.

E8 .... and .... you are now husband and wife according to the witness of the Holy Catholic Church, and the law of the state. Become one. Fulfill your promises. Love and serve the Lord.

What God has united, man must not divide.

F7 Forasmuch as .... and .... have consented together in holy wedlock, and have declared the same before God and in the presence of this company, I pronounce them man and wife, in the name of the Father, and of the Son, and of the Holy Ghost.

What God hath joined together, let not man put asunder.

G6 The minister shall have the man and woman join hands, and then he shall lay his hand upon their hands and say:

.... and .... you have now been joined together in Christian marriage, and I now declare that you are husband and wife according to the witness of the Christian Church and the laws of the state. In the name of the Father, the Son, and the Holy Spirit.

Amen.

H8 I now declare that .... and .... are husband and wife, according to the witness of the Christian Church, and the laws of the state, in the name of the

Father, and the Son, and the Holy Spirit.

What therefore God has joined together, let not man put asunder.

18 Since you have made holy promises to God and to each other, I declare that you are now husband and wife according to the witness of the Christian Church and the law of the state, in the name of the Father, the Son, and the Holy Spirit.

Whom God has joined together, let not man put asunder.

Prayers for the Marriage

The prayers are listed here under four headings, 1. Prayers asking God's Blessing upon the Marriage, 2. Prayers for the Heritage of Children and the Well-Being of Families, 3. Prayers for Spiritual Graces, and 4. Prayers to be Spoken by the Bride and Groom. Numbers and letters are used in this section to refer to the individual prayers. If you decide to combine prayers from different services it is recommended that you use either the traditional wording, or the contemporary wording throughout the prayers. It is rather easy to rewrite prayers using either of the two forms. Your minister can help you with this if you so choose.

Prayers asking God's Blessing upon the Marriage

A5 O eternal God, creator and preserver of all mankind, giver of all spiritual grace, the author of everlasting life, send thy blessing upon these thy servants, this man and this woman, whom we bless in thy name, that they, living faithfully together, may surely perform and keep the vow and covenant betwixt them made, whereof this ring given and received is a token and pledge, and may ever remain in perfect love and peace together, and live according to thy laws, through Jesus Christ our Lord.

B12 O God, who consecrated the state of marriage to be a sign of the spiritual unity between Christ and his Church, bless these your servants, that they may love, honor, and cherish each other in faithfulness and patience, in wisdom and true godliness, and that their home may be a haven of blessing and peace, through Jesus Christ our Lord, who lives and reigns with you and the Holy Spirit, one God, now and forever.

C6 O eternal God, creator and preserver of all mankind, giver of all spiritual grace, the author of everlasting life, send thy blessing upon this man and this woman, whom we bless in thy name, that they may surely perform and keep the vow and covenant between them made, and may ever remain in perfect love and peace together, and live according to thy laws.

Look graciously upon them, that they may love, honor, and cherish each other, and so live together in faithfulness and patience, in wisdom and true godliness, that their home may be a haven of blessing and a place of peace, through Jesus Christ our Lord.

D6 Most merciful and gracious God, of whom the whole family in heaven and earth is named, bestow upon these thy servants the seal of thine approval, and thy fatherly benediction, granting unto them grace to fulfill, with pure and steadfast affection, the vow and covenant between them made. Guide them together, we beseech thee, in the way of righteousness and peace, that loving and serving thee, with one heart and mind, all the days of their life, they may be abundantly enriched with the tokens of thy everlasting favor, in Jesus Christ our Lord.

E7 Eternal God, without your grace no promise is sure. Strengthen .... and .... with the gift of your Spirit, so they may fulfill the vows they have taken. Keep them faithful to each other and to you. Fill them with such love and joy that they may build a home where no one is a stranger, and guide them by your word to serve you all the days of their lives. through Jesus Christ our Lord, to whom be honor and glory forever and ever.

F8 Almighty and most merciful God, who hast now united this man and this woman in the holy estate of matrimony, grant them grace to live therein according to thy holy Word. Strengthen them in constant fidelity and true affection toward each other. Sustain and defend them amidst all trials and temptations, and help them so to pass through this world in faith toward thee, in communion with thy holy Church, and in loving service one of the other, that they may enjoy forever thy heavenly benediction, through Jesus Christ, thy Son our Lord, who liveth and reigneth with thee and the Holy Ghost, one God, world without end.

G7 The couple may kneel and receive the blessing of the pastor and parents.

The Lord God, the creator of the heavens and the earth, who gave life to our first parents and blessed their marriage, bless you that you may grow together in holy love and spend the days of your life praising and glorifying him who loved us and gave himself for us.

Amen.

The parents standing behind the couple may say:

May God's Spirit be upon you to guide you and sustain you, and give you love beyond measure.

L Let us pray for .... and ....

All may pray silently

G9 M Father of love and mercy, pour out your grace upon .... and .... and give them the power of your Spirit, so that they may fulfill with pure hearts and steady faith the vows made here today. Grant them courage for times of testing, endurance for times of trial, strength for times of weakness, but above all a constant love to knit together the heights and depths they will know. Lead them to that joy which only comes through your divine presence in all of life.

Amen.

H7 Eternal God, we ask you to give your divine approval and blessing to .... and .... We pray that they will find through your grace, the power to fulfill their vows, and live together in love and harmony all the days of their life. Guide them through the difficult times, and give them a love that will deepen day by day, and year by year. May faith and holiness be the results of their marriage, that your name and presence will be felt in their home, helping them, guiding their children, and making the way to life eternal, through Jesus Christ our Lord.

19 Eternal God we thank you for life, its wonder and mystery. We thank you for the capacity to share love with one another, and know the joys of that gift you gave us, when you created us in your own image. Father, we pray now for .... and .... that your hand will be upon them, guiding them and leading them through their married life together. Grant them your blessing and your Spirit so that as they walk through the daylight and darkness of life, they may know that strength which only comes from your divine presence.

33 The priest faces the bride and bridegroom and, with hands joined, says:

My dear friends, let us turn to the Lord and pray that he will bless with his grace this woman (or ....) now married in Christ to this man (or ....) and that (through the sacrament of the body and blood of Christ,) he will unite in love the couple he has joined in this holy bond.

All pray silently for a short while. Then the priest extends his hands and continues:

Father, by your power you have made everything out of nothing. In the beginning you created the universe and made mankind in your own likeness. You gave man the constant help of woman so that man and woman should no longer be two, but one flesh, and you teach us that what you have united may never be divided.

Father, you have made the union of man and wife so holy a mystery that it symbolizes the marriage of Christ and his Church.

Father, by your plan man and woman are united, and married life has been established as the one blessing that was not forfeited by original sin or washed away in the flood.

Look with love upon this woman, your daughter, now joined to her husband in marriage. She asks your blessing. Give her the grace of love and peace. May she always follow the example of the holy women whose praises are sung in the scriptures.

May her husband put his trust in her and recognize that she is his equal and the heir with him to the life of grace. May he always honor her and love her as Christ loves his bride, the Church.

Father, keep them always true to your commandments. Keep them faithful in marriage and let them be living examples of Christian life.

Give them the strength which comes from the gospel so that they may be witnesses of Christ to others. (Bless them with children and help them to be good parents. May they live to see their children's children.) And, after a happy old age, grant them fullness of life with the saints in the kingdom of heaven.

(We ask this) through Christ our Lord.

R. Amen.

120 In the following prayer, either the paragraph Holy Father, you created mankind, **or the paragraph** Father, to reveal the plan of your love, **may be omitted, keeping only the paragraph which corresponds to the reading.**

The priest faces the bride and bridegroom and, with hands joined, says:

Let us pray to the Lord for .... and .... who come to God's altar at the beginning of their married life so that they may always be united in love for each other (as now they share in the body and blood of Christ).

All pray silently for a short while. Then the priest extends his hands and continues:

Holy Father, you created mankind in your own image and made man and woman to be joined as husband and wife in union of body and heart and so fulfill their mission in this world.

Father, to reveal the plan of your love, you made the union of husband and wife an image of the covenant between you and your people. In the fulfillment of this sacrament, the marriage of Christian man and woman is a sign of the marriage between Christ and the Church. Father, stretch out your hand, and bless .... and ....

Lord, grant that as they begin to live this sacrament they may share with each other the gifts of your love and become one in heart and mind as witnesses to your presence in their marriage. Help them to create a home together (and give them children to be formed by the gospel and to have a place in your family).

Give your blessings to ...., your daughter, so that she may be a good wife (and mother), caring for the home, faithful in love for her husband, generous and kind.

Give your blessings to ...., your son, so that he may be a faithful husband (and a good father).

Father, grant that as they come together to your table on earth, so they may one day have the joy of sharing your feast in heaven.

(We ask this) through Christ our Lord.

R. Amen.

121 The priest faces the bride and bridegroom and, with hands joined, says:

My dear friends, let us ask God for his continued blessings upon this bridegroom and his bride (or .... and ....).

All pray silently for a short while. Then the priest extends his hands and continues:

Holy Father, creator of the universe, maker of man and woman in your own likeness, source of blessing for married life, we humbly pray to you for this woman who today is united with her husband in this sacrament of marriage.

May your fullest blessing come upon her and her husband so that they may together rejoice in your gift of married love (and enrich your Chruch with their children).

Lord, may they both praise you when they are happy and turn to you in their sorrows. May they be glad that you help them in their work and know that you are with them in their need. May they pray to you in the community of the church, and be your witnesses in the world. May they reach old age in the company of their friends, and come at last to the kingdom of heaven.

(We ask this) through Christ our Lord.

R. Amen.

225 Almighty God, heavenly father of mankind, whose nature is love, look with favor upon this man and this woman who desire now thy blessing upon their vows. We are grateful for the families that have reared them to maturity, the church which has led them to this happy moment. Grant this to be more than an outward union, but rather the blending of hearts and spirits and purposes. Bless each with the inward qualities of loyalty, honor, purity, self-control, trust, cooperation, and forgiveness, that they may keep faithfully this holy covenant, and may live together all their days in true love and perfect peace, through Jesus Christ our Lord.

226 Holy Father, creator of the universe, maker of man and woman in your own likeness, source of blessing for married life, we humbly pray to you for .... and .... who today are united in holy marriage. May your fullest blessing come upon them, so that they may together rejoice in your gift of married love, (**and if it applies**) and enrich your Church with their children. Lord, may they both praise you when they are happy and turn to you in their sorrows. May they be glad that you help them in their work and know that you are with them in their need. May they pray to you in the community of the Church, and be your witnesses in the world. May they reach old age in the company of their friends, and come at last to the kingdom of heaven. We ask this through Jesus Christ our Lord.

Prayers for the Heritage of Children and the Well-Being of Families

A6 O Almighty God, creator of mankind, who only art the well-spring of life, bestow upon these thy servants, if it be thy will, the gift and heritage of children, and grant that they may see their children brought up in thy faith and fear, to the honor and glory of thy name, through Jesus Christ our Lord.

B9 Almighty God, Creator of mankind, the source of all life, grant to .... and .... , if it be your will, the gift and heritage of children, and the grace to nurture them in the knowledge and love of your name, through Jesus Christ our Lord.

F9 O Almighty God, creator of mankind, who only art the well-spring of life, bestow upon these thy servants, if it by thy will, the gift and heritage of children, and grant that they may see their children brought up in thy faith and fear, to the honor and glory of thy name, through Jesus Christ our Lord.

F10 O God, who art our dwelling place in all generations, look with favor upon the homes of our land. Enfold husbands and wives, parents and children, in the bonds of thy pure love, and so bless our homes, that they may be a shelter for the defenseless, a bulwark for the tempted, a resting place for the weary, and a foretaste of our eternal home in thee, through Jesus Christ our Lord.

G10 L Let us pray for all the families of the earth.

All may pray silently

M Eternal God, in your wisdom you have given us families for our refuge and strength here on earth. We pray for all the families of the earth, and especially those families gathered here today. Remind us of the bonds which unite us and the high goals you set before us. Deliver us from every evil which will tear us apart, and strengthen every good impulse that our family life will be stronger, and that children will know a foretaste of your love and devotion, through the shared love and faith of a mother and a father. These prayers we ask in the name of Jesus Christ our Lord. Amen.

Prayers for Spiritual Graces

A7 O God, who hast so consecrated the state of matrimony that in it is represented the spiritual marriage and unity betwixt Christ and his Church, look mercifully upon these thy servants, that they may love, honor, and cherish each other, and so live together in faithfulness and patience, in wisdom and true godliness, that their home may be a haven of blessing and of peace, through the same Jesus Christ our Lord, who liveth and reigneth with thee and the Holy Spirit ever one God, world without end.

B8 Almighty God, look graciously, we pray, on this man and this woman, and on all whom you make to be one flesh in holy marriage. Make their lives together a sacrament of your love to this broken world, so that unity may overcome estrangement, forgiveness heal guilt, and joy triumph over despair, in the name of our Lord Jesus Christ, to whom be all honor and glory, now and forever.

B10 Almighty God, giver of life and love, bless .... and .... whom you have joined in holy matrimony. Grant them wisdom and devotion in the ordering of their common life that each may be to the other a strength in need, a counselor in perplexity, a comfort in sorrow, and a companion in joy. And so knit their wills together in your will, and their spirits in your Spirit, that they may live together in love and peace all the days of their life, through Jesus Christ our Lord.

B11 Almighty God, by whose love the whole world is created, sustained and redeemed, so fill .... and .... with the overflowing abundance of your grace that their lives may reflect your compassion for all men. May their love for each other not blind them to the brokenness in the world. As you teach them to bind up each other's wounds, teach them also to heal the hurts of others. As their mutual respect orders their common life within the family, direct them to their share also in the shaping of a society in which human dignity may flourish and abound. At all times and in all seasons may they rejoice to serve you and to give you thanks, through Jesus Christ our Lord.

G8 The couple stands. The minister, a lector, or one of the wedding party may offer the biddings for the following prayer.

L Let us give thanks to God for his gifts and his goodness to us today.

All may pray silently

M Lord God, we give you praise and thanksgiving for all your gifts. We thank you that you created us, gave us the breath of life, and the abiltiy to be one with another in faithfulness and in love. We thank you for the love that has been formed in the hearts of .... and .... Let your hand be upon them so that their love will grow and bloom as a flower in your kingdom. Amen.

I12 For these prayers and intentions we ask your divine benediction. Help us all make our lives true temples of your Spirit. We pray your blessing upon every home which has led to the founding of this new marriage. May we all stand under your love and direction that we will help .... and .... to know the joy and wonder of life within your divine purposes, through Jesus Christ our Lord.

Prayers by the Bride and Groom

I10 Eternal God, help me to be a Christian man and a loving husband. Make firm in my life the vows of marriage, that I may walk in your will and be the person you would have me be.

I11 Heavenly Father, guide me and help me to be the Christian person you would have me be, so that I will be a loving wife in the years ahead. So bless our home that all will know that you are our heavenly Father.

201 O God, our Father in heaven, we now kneel before you very happy, but somewhat nervous. We feel you brought us together in the beginning, helped our love to grow, and at this moment are with us in a special way. We ask that you stay by our side in the days ahead. Protect us from anything which might harm this marriage, give us courage when burdens come our way, teach us to forgive one another when we fail.

202 I ask from you the assistance I need to be a good husband and father. Never let me take my wife for granted or forget she needs to be loved. If you bless us with children, I promise to love them, to care for them, to give them the best possible example.

203 I ask from you the assistance I need to be a good wife and mother. May I never forget how important my husband's work is for his happiness or fail to give him encouragement. If you bless me with motherhood, I promise to give myself totally to the children, even to the point of stepping aside when they must walk alone.

204 We ask, finally, that in our old age we may love one another as deeply and cherish each other as much as we do at this very moment. May you grant these wishes which we offer through your Son, Jesus Christ our Lord and Savior.

Benedictions

A9, B13, and C7 God the Father, God the Son, God the Holy Ghost/Spirit, bless, preserve, and keep you. The Lord mercifully with his favor look upon you, and fill you with all spiritual benediction and grace, that ye/you may so live together in this life, that in the world to come ye/you may have life everlasting. Amen.

D8 The Lord bless you and keep you. The Lord make his face to shine upon you and be gracious unto you. The Lord lift up his countenance upon you and give you peace. Amen.

E9 Glory be to him who can keep you from falling and bring you safe to his glorious presence, innocent and happy. To God, the only God, who saves us through Jesus Christ our Lord, be the glory, majesty, authority, and power, which he had before time began, now and forever. Amen.

E10 The grace of the Lord Jesus Christ, the love of God, and the fellowship of the Holy Spirit, be with you all. Amen.

F11 and H9 The Lord bless thee/you and keep thee/you. The Lord make his face to shine upon thee/you, and be gracious unto thee/you. The Lord lift up his countenance upon thee/you, and give thee/you peace, both now and forevermore. Amen.

F12 God Almighty send you hs light and truth to keep you all the days of your life. The hand of God protect you, his holy angels accompany you. God the Father, God the Son, and God the Holy Ghost, cause his grace to be mighty upon you. Amen.

G11 All present will join in the Lord's Prayer.

May the blessings of God almighty be with you. Amen.

May he give you his peace. Amen.

May God the Father, the Son, and the Holy Spirit keep you and sustain you all the days of your life. Amen.

I13 Now to him who by the power at work within us is able to do far more abundantl, than all that we ask or think, to him be glory in the Church and in Christ Jesus to all generations, forever and ever. Amen.

I25 God the eternal Father keep you in love with each other, so that the peace of Christ may stay with you and be always in your home.

R. Amen.

May (your children bless you,) your friends console you, and all men live in peace with you.

R. Amen.

May you always bear witness to the love of God in this world so that the afflicted and the needy will find in you generous friends, and welcome you into the joys of heaven.

R. Amen.

And may almighty God bless you all, the Father, and the Son, + and the Holy Spirit.

R. Amen.

127 May the Lord Jesus, who was a guest at the wedding in Cana, bless you and your families and friends.

R. Amen.

May Jesus, who loved his Church to the end, always fill your hearts with his love.

R. Amen.

May he grant that, as you believe in his resurrection, so you may wait for him in joy and hope.

R. Amen.

And may almighty God bless you all, the Father, and the Son, + and the Holy Spirit.

R. Amen.

227 Grace be to you and peace from God our Father and the Lord Jesus Christ. Amen.

228 May the peace of God, which passes all understanding, keep your hearts and minds in Christ Jesus. Amen.

229 Now to him who is able to keep you from falling and to present you faultless before the presence of his glory with rejoicing, to the only God, our savior through Jesus Christ our Lord, be glory, majesty, dominion, and authority before all time and now and forever. Amen.

230 May the blessings of God almighty, the Father, the Son, and the Holy Spirit be with you and guide you both now and forever more. Amen.

MUSIC FOR WORSHIP AND WEDDINGS

The music used at a wedding is to be music appropriate to the worship of God. The old hymn says, "Give of your best to the master," and this should be your standard for the music you select. A wedding service is not a reception. If you have a favorite "hit tune," or theme from a motion picture, etc., have this played or sung at the reception. The music used for worship need not be excessively formal nor complicated, but it must point to the majesty and dignity of the God who has created us.

Listed below is a good variety of music which is appropriate for marriage services. It includes hymns and solos. You may want to speak with your organist and arrange to hear what the various peices sound like, so you can best determine how they will fit into your service. This list is just a small selection, and there is great room for variety andf creativi just in selecting the music for your wedding. Your church hymnal is also a good resource for you to consult.

It is only proper that you consult with your minister and obtain his approval of the music you select.

Preludes

Cantabile	Franck
Wedding Music, Volume I	(Concordia)
Prelude in D Major	Fischer
Adagio (Occasional Oratorio)	Handel
Aria in F Major	Handel
Cantilena	Rheinberger
Air from "Water Music Suite"	Handel
Rhosymedre	R. Vaughn Williams
Suite Gothique	Boellmann
Toccata and Fugue in D Minor	Bach
If Thou But Suffer God to Guide Thee	Bach
Choral in E	Franck
Choral in A Minor	Franck

Prelude in Classic Style (Contemporary)	Young
Panis Angelicus	Franck
Now Thank We All Our God	Karg-Elert
Chimes Preludes	Holler

Processionals

Processional March	Guilmant
Wedding Music, Volume I	(Concordia)
Aria in F Major	Handel
Processional	Handel
Air from "Water Music Suite"	Handel
Wedding March	Schreiner
Psalm XX	Marcello
Psalm XIX	Marcello

Solos

O Perfect Love	Barnby
The Greatest of These is Love	Bitgood
Wedding Prayer	Dunlap
Wither Thou Goest	Cassler
Be Thou But Near	Bach
The Lord's Prayer	Malotte
Rejoice in the Lord Alway	Purcell
Eternal Life (Prayer of St. Francis)	Duggan
O Savior, Hear Me!	Gluck
(Flute or Violin with this is most appropriate)	
I'll Walk with God	Brodszky
One Hand, One Heart	Bernstein

Hymns

Joyful, Joyful We Adore Thee	Beethoven
O Love Divine	Dykes
Jesus, Thou Joy of Loving Hearts	Baker
Lead Us Heavenly Father, Lead Us	Edmeston
Now Thank We All Our God	Cruger
Love Divine, All Loves Excelling	Zundel
Praise Ye the Lord, the Almighty	Neander
Praise, My Soul, the King of Heaven	Goss

The King of Love My Shepherd Is	Dykes
Be Thou My Vision	Slane

There are many other hymns which are appropriate and they can be used often as solos, as well as processionals and recessionals.

Recessionals

Toccata, "Thou art the Rock"	Mulet
Wedding Music, Volume I	(Concordia)
Toccata in F Major	Buxtehude
Trumpet Tune in D	Purcell
Trumpet Voluntary in D	Purcell
Psalm XIX	Marcello
Choral Song	Wesley
Allegro from Suite Gothique	Boellmann
Rigaudon	Campra
Trumpet Air	Cook
Joyful, Joyful We Adore Thee	Young (Contemporary)
Toccata	Young
Toccata	Peeters

ACKNOWLEDGEMENTS

The following is a list of sources used in preparing this manual. Sincere gratitude is extended to the men and women who, through the moving of God's Spirit in their lives, produced the materials, and also gratitude is extended to the publishers and owners of copyrights who gave their permission to use them.

The Book of Common Prayer, according to the use of the Protestant Episcopal Church in the United States of America, New York: The Seabury Press, 1953.

The Book of Common Worship, Provisional Services, prepared by the Joint Committee on Worship for the Cumberland Presbyterian Church, the Presbyterian Church in the United States, and the United Presbyterian Church in the United States of America, Philadelphia: The Westminster Press, 1966.

The Book of Worship for Church and Home, The United Methodist Church, Nashville: The Methodist Publishing House, 1965.

The Cokesbury Marriage Manual, ed. William H. Leach, Nashville: Abingdon Press, 1945.

The Holy Bible, Revised Standard Version, New York: Division of Christian Education of the National Council of Churches of Christ in the U.S.A., 1946-1952.

The Marriage Service, prepared by the Inter-Lutheran Commission on Worship for provisional use, (Contemporary Worship 3) Philadelphia: Board of Publications, Lutheran Church in America, 1972.

Rite of Marriage, The Roman Ritual, Copyright © 1969, International Committee on English in the Liturgy, Inc., Toronto. All rights reserved.

The Minister's Service Handbook, James L. Christensen, New York: Fleming H. Revell Co., 1960.

Service Book and Hymnal, The Commission on Liturgy and Hymnal of the Lutheran Church in America and the American Lutheran Church, Minneapolis: Augusburg Publishing House, 1958.

Services for Trial Use, Authorized Alternatives to Prayer Book Services, New York: The Church Hymnal Corporation, 1971.

Together for Life, Joseph M. Champlin, Notre Dame, Indiana: Ave Maria Press, 1970, source for the Prayer of the Couple and Prayer of the Faithful in the Roman Catholic Service. Used by permission.

The Worshipbook, prepared by the Joint Committee on Worship for the Cumberland Presbyterian Church, the Presbyterian Church in the United States, and the United Presbyterian Church in the United States of America, Philadelphia: The Westminster Press, 1970.